Marriage Masterclass

Dedicated jointly to

Dave and Joyce Ames, whose original vision for marriage enrichment has now spanned four decades. Their faithfulness and dedication set the standards for marriage ministry and has impacted on the lives of thousands of couples worldwide. We are far from alone in being indebted to them.

And to the Trustees – present and recent – of Mission to Marriage: Christian Marriage Ministries: Malcolm, Peter, Tom, Gordon, Rachael, Bryan and Iain. Their help, enthusiasm and unfailing support have enabled us to take over the mantle passed on by Dave and Joyce.

Marriage Masterclass

An interactive resource about overcoming
obstacles to a great marriage

Dr Tony & Anne Hobbs

Authentic
LIFESTYLE

First printed in 2002 by Authentic Lifestyle
08 07 06 05 04 03 02   7 6 5 4 3 2 1

Authentic Lifestyle is an imprint of Authentic Media,
P.O. Box 300, Carlisle, Cumbria, CA3 0QS, UK
and
P.O. Box 1047, Waynesboro, GA 30830-2047, USA
www.paternoster-publishing.com

British Library Cataloguing in Publication Data
A catalogue record for this book is available from the British
Library

ISBN 1-85078-456-6

Cover Design by Paul Lewis
Typeset by WestKey Ltd, Falmouth, Cornwall
Printed in Great Britain by Cox & Wyman, Reading, RG1 8EX

Contents

Introduction and the Divorce that Never Was

Not just *why* and *what*, but *how*.

This book is about overcoming obstacles; things that get in the way of you having a great marriage. Generally, Christians know what the Bible says about marriage. Although some of us may not be too sure about, for example, some of the details about marriage in the Old Testament law, or exactly how we should interpret what Jesus says about divorce, nevertheless the basic principles about marriage are pretty clear. However, simply understanding them, or reminding ourselves of them afresh will not make our marriage better. *For most Christians, the need is not for more information about the Biblical principles of marriage but how to put these principles into practice.* Frankly, for most of us there is a significant gap between the Biblical ideal of marriage and our own experience of marriage. Or to put it another way, there are blocks or obstacles that get in the way of us living out what we know. After a while these blocks can seem insurmountable. The main aim of this book is to help you to tackle afresh the obstacles you've encountered.

Christian teaching that only talks about *why* and *what* is not enough; genuine Biblical teaching also considers the *how?* So while this book encourages you to consider the *whys* and *whats*, there is also a great emphasis on *how*.

This book was not written in a vacuum. It is the product of marriage teaching and counselling that has helped thousands of couples for over a quarter of a century. The teaching was originated in the UK primarily for UK Christians. The organisation, known throughout most of its history as Mission to Marriage, has always emphasised certain operating principles:

- the teaching is explicitly Biblical
- the teaching is designed to help couples experience better marriages, even if one partner is not a Christian
- the approach to teaching is non-pressurised, helping people to work through issues in a mature and enriching way. It does not put them under psychological pressure or generate guilt
- couples are enabled to talk to each other about core issues and problems in an encouraging and uplifting way

These operating principles are very much part of this book. Each chapter discusses the Biblical principles about a specific topic, with the aim of helping you overcome any particular obstacles you may be experiencing. There are points for reflection, encouraging you to think through the topic at a pace with which you feel comfortable. There are also specific questions related to each topic. If both partners are able to read the book together then it's helpful to discuss your answers to the questions. But if, for whatever reason, your partner isn't reading the book, you can still benefit from doing the questions solo. For the questions to be of genuine value, it is important that one partner doesn't try and use them as a weapon against the other! This is particularly important if you are married to a non-Christian. The issues discussed in this book will still be of value to you and your marriage but you may need to find appropriately gentle ways of communicating them to your partner. One important principle which we observe in marriage counselling is that although both partners may be committed to wanting to improve the marriage and addressing specific problem issues, it does not mean that both can work through the issues at the same pace. Just because one partner needs to move at a slower pace doesn't necessarily mean they are less committed.

The divorce that never was

This book is called *Marriage Masterclass* because we nearly got divorced! Like virtually every new couple we approached married life with enthusiasm and optimism, with real expectations of a near perfect marriage. We had grounds for our optimism. We had known each other for a long time as good friends; we were not immature teenagers or even still in our early twenties; we'd both done several years of counselling training; most importantly, we were strong evangelical Christians determined to base our lives and marriage on Biblical principles. We both had experience of Christian leadership and were expected by others to have important leadership roles in the future church. But a week before our seventh wedding anniversary we separated and lived apart for well over two years. Although at first we had hoped and prayed for reconciliation, eventually we became convinced that our marriage was over. With some reluctance, a solicitor was approached about divorce proceedings. We saw this not as the next step but a legal recognition of what we perceived had already happened: the marriage had irrevocably broken down. Divorce was a survival strategy, a way of drawing a line under a painful and awful period.

We didn't know it at the time, but throughout this period God had been working in each of our lives in special ways; first breaking, then healing. He used the divorce papers to force us to meet and talk. The next few weeks were as ghastly as any that had gone before but in a different way. We realised that if our commitment to the Lord was to be real, then uncomfortable Biblical principles had to be lived out. We knew we had to consider reconciliation even though we thought it hopeless. A few months later, still not really desiring reconciliation, we came back together. This involved job changes, house moves and leaving churches where we'd received love and support during our time apart. We felt as if we had cast ourselves adrift in an open boat and we weren't sure if we liked our only companion very much! Certainly we were reluctant to trust one another – not a good feeling.

It would be romantic to report that suddenly everything was wonderful. In truth the process of reconciliation was difficult and painful. Hour after painful hour was necessarily spent talking and sharing with each other, going over and reliving terrible memories and experiences. Trust was gradually rebuilt. It took another two years before we could genuinely say to each other 'I love you' and mean it without reservation.

One of our prayers during that time was that the pain of getting back together would have wider value. We began to think that maybe we could help other people in the church who were going through marriage problems; not because we had all the answers but because we had some sense of the pain of marriage difficulties. Such a pastoral care role began to emerge, but at that point we would have been stunned to discover how far it would go.

Some years later, after we had been happily together for longer than we'd been married prior to our separation, we unexpectedly came across an advertisement for Mission to Marriage. We'd never heard of the organisation, although we later discovered that it had been founded by Dave and Joyce Ames over a quarter of a century earlier. It was, depending on how one counts, the biggest of the Christian marriage ministry organisations in the UK. The advertisement was for a couple to take over the running of the ministry when Dave and Joyce retired. We had a nagging sense that we should find out more, even though the timing and circumstances appeared, at first sight, to be all wrong. But take over we did. At first we were very reluctant to share about our period of separation. We didn't want to keep it a secret but we didn't want it to get in the way of the excellent teaching programme that had been so carefully honed over the years by Dave and Joyce; teaching that had made a major impact on thousands of people across the UK and other parts of the world. However, when we gradually began to share about our past difficulties, we found the opposite effect. In some ways it gave the teaching a new credibility. People appreciated that we knew what it was like to have marriage problems. So now at the beginning of our seminar and conference teaching we make three introductory points:

- we are in marriage ministry not because we've had a perfect marriage but because at one point we got things very, very wrong.
- had we experienced and implemented the Mission to Marriage teaching early in our marriage we could have avoided many of our most serious mistakes.
- we can testify that even when the marriage seems hopeless, God can rebuild it: not patch it up but genuinely make things better than we could imagine possible.

This book is a marriage masterclass not because we, the writers, have always got things right but because we'd like to share from painful experience how to overcome obstacles and blocks that get in the way of marriage being what God wants it to be. We know the principles work.

Hopes and Expectations:
Coming to Terms with Reality
or Bringing about Change?

Before we get into specific marriage issues, it may be helpful to
unearth some thoughts, assumptions and attitudes that may be
lurking in our subconscious minds. Then, slowly and gently, we
can begin to consider the implications of change.

Some introductory questions

If possible, spend a few moments reflecting on a few questions.
You might find it helpful to keep your answers in mind as you
read what follows.

1. Think back to your childhood. Can you remember what your
   thoughts were about growing up and getting married? Did
   you:
   (a) Expect to get married?
   (b) Expect to be happily married?
   (c) Have a mental picture of what your future partner would
       look like and what they would be like?
2. Think back to what were probably early teenage years, the
   time when you first really started to be aware of the opposite
   sex. Did you:
   (a) Expect to get married?
   (b) Have a fairly clear-cut idea of what you thought married
       life would be?

(c) What hopes did you have about your future partner?

Throughout this book we'll be speaking of 'partner'. This is not intended to undermine the importance of marriage but constantly putting 'husband or wife' looks clumsy and the term 'spouse' never seems to be very user-friendly term.

The disappointment of reality?

Unless we grew up determined to remain single, from a very early age most of us had an expectation of a happy marriage. This hope and expectation may have begun at a very young age, worked out in children's games such as 'mothers and fathers'. However, typically such games reflect children's actual observations of their own parents. A domineering wife may be observed in her daughter's playing wife to a boy 'husband' whom she will, in turn, expect to domineer – even if in other games he is an obviously strong character. The more sophisticated versions of the game will incorporate the children's observations of other role models, such as husbands and wives on television. Thus from early years the child is involved in tension which may go un-noted; the childhood notion of the hope of a happy marriage but where the early role play of marriage and family life reflects the realism of role models that they have observed.

As we continued to grow, such games were left behind as both future hopes and present observations became more sophisticated. What was perceived as good and desirable behaviour from parental role models became incorporated in expectations, while at the same time unattractive or undesirable behaviour was excluded. To use the girl as an example, this may have resulted, at the extremes, in:

I want to be like my mother and marry someone like my father.

Or: I do not want to be like my mother nor marry someone like my father.

Or, more often:

I want to be like my mother in these respects but unlike her in other respects.

So – to give examples from the boy's perspective: the boy who sees his father acting in a loving way towards his wife may resolve to copy such behaviour when he gets married; the boy who sees his father beating his wife may be determined not to be a husband like his father.

Of course the above are greatly simplified examples and the issues about the child's psychological development and their expectation of their future role as husband or wife are considerably more complex. What we want to underline here is that hopes and expectations about future marriage go hand in hand with observations made over many years – which usually involve awareness of desirable and undesirable elements.

As the child moves from puberty into the emotional and bio-chemical turmoil of teenage years, early relationships with members of the opposite sex will be based, often with hesitancy and naivety, on how others conduct relationships. At this point the hope may go no further than to have a boyfriend or girl-friend; the overwhelming ideal is about having a relationship with someone who is willing to have a relationship! The teenage experiences of pre-adult relationships are usually based on activities, such as doing things together within acceptable peer group norms. Although in biological years the two teenagers are closer to adulthood, in terms of living out a relationship they are in fact further removed from the roles of husband and wife than were the boy and girl innocently playing at mothers and fathers. The teenage couple's exploration of what it means to be a couple will focus upon activity and in particular the physical aspects of relationship. This will tend to exclude the routine of life, such as how to relate to one another when it's time to do the weekly food shopping. So while the teenager may discover helpful information about some aspects of relating to the opposite sex, there may be little in the relationship to challenge and refine the expectations of a future marriage partner that became a firm part of the subconscious years earlier. The teenage hopes will generally be focused on adult freedom: 'When we have a home of our own …'; 'When I don't have to be in by 10 o'clock …'; 'When we have money to do the things we want to do …' In other words, hopes that are about doing rather than being.

The adult (or late teenager) entering into marriage will do so with a suitcase full of hopes and expectations. For individuals with mental illness or certain counselling needs these may be negative but for most people the hopes and expectations will be positive. In essence the forthcoming marriage will be seen as:

- the fulfilment of hopes and expectations nurtured over many years. This is the same type of hope as when, as a child, they spent December imagining unwrapping the presents on Christmas morning.
- the marriage partner conforming to their dream ideal. If they are not immediately recognisable as such, part of the hope and expectation is that marriage will turn them into that ideal.
- a time of positive life change; for example, the opportunity to leave the parental home and authority.

The hopes and expectations may survive a literal and meta-phorical honeymoon period. But reality quickly sets in and it becomes obvious that life has changed. Some of it may be a surprise and perhaps emotionally uncomfortable. Psycho-logically what happens is often some form of dissonance where there is a tension between ideal and reality. There are a variety of different ways of coping with this inner tension. Some of the more common ones are:

- to assume that it's just teething troubles and that, given time, the ideal will happen.
- doubts about whether the partner was the correct choice.
- blaming oneself; assuming 'I must be doing something wrong.' (A common response from newly married wives.)
- trying to ignore the problem, often becoming involved in ex-ternal distractions. (A common response from newly-married husbands.)
- blaming external circumstances, especially lack of financial resources.

- shifting the hopes and expectations into a new future situation: 'When we are more used to living together' or 'When we have children'.

If a crisis is avoided, another coping strategy kicks in; the apparently adult assessment that the hopes and expectations were childish ideals and that they need to be packed away along with dolls, teddy bears and train sets. Marriage becomes more 'realistic' and what were personal ideals are now experienced only in romantic films and books. At best, the marriage has entered a rut where hopes and expectations are revised downwards. At worst, poison begins a slow drip-feed into the marriage, beginning with disappointment and ending in blaming oneself or the partner for not living up to the ideal. This leaves open the possibility of a perverted form of the original ideal reoccurring; that it might be better to end the relationship and try to find someone else who will conform more closely to the ideal. A variation of this is to enter into an affair with someone because they look as though they might fulfil the ideal.

Change in relationships:
a distant hope or an uncomfortable reality?

In a limited sense, putting away ideals may be healthy. The hopes and expectations held by each partner may be childish and immature, incapable of being translated into the adult world. But instead of being packed away in the attic with the once-loved teddy bear, they need re-examining with adult wisdom and insight. When we look at the Biblical expectations of marriage, we discover not that our hopes and expectations are too big and unrealistic but that they aren't big enough. Our hopes and expectations, when honestly examined, turn out to be hopes for a mutually acceptable contractual partnership with another person. By contrast, the Scriptural expectation is a covenant that results in our becoming one flesh with another person. All this raises a host of questions and issues that we

shall address throughout the rest of the book. But first we need
to believe that it is possible to get out of even the deepest rut.
This is not about trying to convince ourselves of something that
we don't really think is true: it is about a deliberate recognition that change is possible. For the Christian, this change can
be divinely prompted and divinely empowered. We must
continue to apply adult rigour to this, and not slip back into
childish hopes that treat God more as Father Christmas than
Lord. Change may be very uncomfortable at first. In the
early stages we may long to go back to how things were: the
familiarity and comfort of the known.

We kid ourselves if we think change is easy. The more important the change, the more psychologically uncomfortable it is
likely to be. After such change has taken place, we may look back
and wonder what it was that so frightened us or caused us concern – hindsight is easy. Before change happens, or during the
early stages of the change process, the *status quo* seems very
attractive. As a way of thinking about this Biblically, we'll reflect
on a time of change from the Old Testament. It's not a passage
that explicitly has anything to do with marriage, but the principles about change in the passage relate directly to our married
lives.

Deuteronomy 11:11–17: a Time of Change

After forty years of desert wanderings the Israelites are poised
to enter the Promised Land, the land promised hundreds of
years earlier to Abraham (Genesis 12:1–3). For much of the
period the Israelites had been in Egypt, most of it as slaves.
Common sense tells us, and the early chapters of Exodus
confirm, that this was a time of great unhappiness for the Israelites, and they longed for change. The promise of a land of their
own was inevitably the focus for all their hopes, but the hope
remained a distant one. For decades and centuries this distant
hope had no impact on everyday life, which was spent pleasing
their Egyptian masters.

During the same time Egyptian society was a stable one and would remain so for hundreds of years, the Exodus apart. The years of famine, when Joseph managed the Egyptian economy (Genesis 37–50), were so devastating to the Egyptians because they had little experience of dealing with problems and disaster. The geography of Egypt made it a highly stable place. While it would be an exaggeration to say Egypt was cut off from the rest of the world, Egypt had little need of interaction with the rest of the region. It was not an area through which people naturally passed. It was a geographical terminus. Consequently, it was not an easy country to invade. Its military forces were formidable and its geographical features made it difficult for foreign powers to consider any campaign against it. Within Egypt, stability was the foundation of society, the basis of what we'd call 'their world view.' The greatest eulogy a deceased Pharaoh could have was that nothing changed during his reign; quite a contrast to modern political manifestos! Crucial to all this was the weather and the Nile. In one sense Egypt is a desert where it doesn't rain. What prevents it from being an uninhabitable wasteland is the Nile. The great and reliable river forms the geographical and social backbone of Egypt. A modern-day map of Egypt highlights this, with towns and settlements all the way along the Nile and the rest of the map being little more than blank space. The Egyptians had no hope of rain because it didn't rain. They relied exclusively on the Nile and its tributaries for all their water. They could do so because the Nile was a totally reliable river, unlike the two great rivers of Mesopotamia, the Tigris and Euphrates. The Nile gently flooded in a predictable way every year, and agriculture was managed accordingly. The flooding of the Tigris and Euphrates was unpredictable, and once or twice every couple of centuries both would flood *in extremis*, wiping out towns and villages. The Egyptians knew nothing of such floods. One of the many features of this stability was that Egyptian society was not nomadic, like many people groups in the Ancient Near East. Abraham's descendants had originally been nomads who had settled in Egypt. In times of famine elsewhere, Egypt was the sensible place to go, not just for the nomads in the Canaan area but for people throughout the region. Nomads move to find water and grazing for their animals. In Egypt such movement that there was took place only along the Nile banks. There was no point in looking for water and grazing elsewhere, because there was none; but no matter, for the Nile and its immediate vicinity offered both in abundance. We can also note in passing that the plagues brought by Moses, traumatic in themselves, were more so for the Egyptians because many of them struck at the very foundations of Egyptian life.

The limitation for Egyptian society was that land more than a few hundred feet away from the Nile required irrigation to make it usable. Similarly any project, such as building, that needed water meant it had to be brought from the Nile. There were no local cisterns built to collect rain because there was no rain. We labour the point because those of us who live in a country where rain is frequent need to make a conscious effort to imagine life without rain. Moving water is hard work and irrigation is labour intensive. The Egyptians were not unduly bothered by this constraint however, as they had an ample supply of slave labour in the form of the Israelites. The slavery of the Israelites had, within a few centuries, become part of the bedrock of the *status quo*, the stability and unchanging nature, of Egyptian culture. To let them go, even temporarily, had become unthinkable for the Egyptians.

But go they did. God intervened and through Moses the people were led out of Egypt; or as the Hebrew puts it, up from Egypt, which offers a psychological aspect missing from the English. The departure resulted in major change not only for the Egyptians but also for the Israelites. Although life in Egypt fell far short of the Israelites' hopes, it did have one significant psychological advantage; they too benefited from the known and the familiar. Life may not have been as physically comfortable as they would have liked but it was psychologically secure. Their mental comfort zones were very clearly defined. Nevertheless, the hope of freedom and expectations about a land of their own were supremely powerful and they left Egypt. Without implying any theological parallels, this experience is remarkably like aspects of a modern wedding. They prepared to leave the home where they had grown up; they prepared for the change with a special meal; they began their new life with a journey – and although the desert wilderness was hardly a honeymoon location, it was a honeymoon experience! But not unlike many couples' experience of honeymoons, doubts and uncertainties set in quickly. Immediate fears dominated their thinking (Exodus 14:11,12). Even though they came through the fears unscathed and move into a time of rejoicing (Exodus 15:1–20), the new life was not the dream scenario for which they had hoped. Pessimistic reality became a companion on their journey, a pessimism that had been around for some time. From the very beginning of the change process, before the first plague, the Israelites began to regret the cost of change and sought to revert back to the comfort of the familiar (Exodus 5:21). It is obvious from the books of Exodus and Numbers that after the first heady taste of freedom, the Israelites found the change process very difficult. Once they left Egypt, the uncertainty of food and water was a totally new experience for them; nothing in their lives to date had equipped them to deal with this and the new life to which they had been called. The long centuries of hope and expectations were blown away by the uncomfortable nature of change.

Pause and reflect

At this point, pause and reflect. How did your early experience of marriage compare to your hopes and expectations now? Can you relate to the attitude of the Israelites as they left Egypt? If so, think about how you coped at the time and whether how you coped was helpful for the longer term.

Back to the desert

With the wisdom of hindsight, we know that the difficult time the Israelites had in the desert wilderness could have been short-term. Had they persisted with living outside their comfort zones and been truly committed to doing what God had said, then they could have moved into the Promised Land very quickly. But doubts and fears continued to dominate over the hopes and expectations. What should have been a short-term period turns into a stay in the desert wilderness lasting nearly forty years. (See Numbers chapters 13 and 14.) For that first generation of Israelites out of Egypt, the desert becomes the norm of everyday life. They have been redeemed from slavery in Egypt but cannot enter into the hope of the Promised Land. We can imagine that many of those Israelites came to terms with their situation by rationalising that their original hopes and expectations were unrealistic, even childish, and had to be put away forever.

Pause and reflect

Once again, reflect upon whether this is in any way similar to your marriage situation. Has your reality fallen far short of your original hopes and expectations? Has your response been to 'come to terms with reality' and to allow the original hopes to wither and fade away? Are you not as pleased and joyful with married life as you'd secretly like to be and have you resigned yourself to believing that this is all it can be?

Into the Promised Land

Perhaps the Israelites had given up. God hadn't. At the end of the period during which the Israelites had learnt more about God and more about themselves than they perhaps realised at the time, the hopes and expectations are once again within their grasp. Moses' successor, Joshua, is chosen by God to lead the Israelites into the Promised Land. We need to be brutally honest here. This is not an account of the Israelites having a change of heart, putting their faith in God and everything suddenly going very well. Once again their challenge is to operate outside their comfort zones. Possession of the Promised Land is not simply a stroll across the border and a putting up of their tents. They have to get involved in battles and hardships. Things might have been very different had they had the faith to go in forty years earlier, but Scripture does not tell us what might have been. The battles and difficulties last a long time but they are worth all the effort. After four centuries in Egypt and four decades in the desert, they have come home to the land promised by God to Abraham.

Pause and Reflect

Are you content with your marriage? Are you content for your hopes and expectations to remain unfulfilled dreams? Are you prepared to be involved in change for the better, even if such change is uncomfortable and difficult at first? Being involved in such change is more than merely reading the remaining chapters of this book; it is about using them to put into practice Biblical principles. Ideally the change will be something both you and your partner commit to together. However, the challenge may need to start with you as an individual. The first discomfort you may need to come to terms with might be that you want change for the better while your partner is content with the *status quo*.

Questions

1. With mature consideration:
    (a) What hopes and expectations that you had/have about marriage were really founded on childish thinking?
    (b) What hopes and expectations that you had/have about marriage remain valid even if unfulfilled?

2. (a) What do you think could change for the better in your marriage if one or both of you were committed to change?
    (b) What would you like to change for the better in your marriage? How could you bring about such change?
    (c) What do you think God's perspective is on the above answers?

3. How willing are you to change? How willing are you to move outside your present comfort zone?

Communication

Point to ponder:

Effective communication is not saying something as well as possible but ensuring that the person with whom you are communicating understands exactly what you mean.

The three levels of communication in marriage

Communication is vitally important. In fact communication could be described as the life blood of any relationship. We communicate on several different levels. First there is the basic, pragmatic level of practical exchanges, things such as: 'What shall we have for tea tonight?', 'I'll be late home', 'Where shall we go for our holiday?' Then there is a deeper level where we talk, discuss and exchange ideas. Friendships are usually formed and flourish at this level and this type of communication is an important component in a healthy marriage. The pitfall is that we might be lulled into believing that we really know our partner when what we actually know are their thoughts and ideas on a variety of subjects. The deepest level of communication is the most difficult; the open, honest exchange of feelings. The principle reason that this is the most difficult is because it can seem the most scary; to do it at all involves making ourselves vulnerable. This is where we take risks in the relationship. It has been known for couples who have been married for many years, who on the surface have very happy marriages, to realise that they have never actually communicated on this deepest level. This is where we really get to know one another and this is where the living as one becomes a reality. Although at first it is the scariest level of communication, it is also the most rewarding, leading to greater intimacy and understanding. However, it is a level of communication that needs to be worked at, as it doesn't come naturally to most couples in our society.

When our partner does talk about feelings it is important we react accordingly. This means with appropriate sensitivity! If someone is talking subjectively, on a feelings level, they will not usually welcome objective comments, however helpful and well-intentioned those comments are intended to be. Giving objective feedback to someone who is sharing on a subjective level will tend to make them feel devalued. They need to know that their feelings are understood, respected, possibly empathised with. Just listening sympathetically is often the best thing that a partner can do. Once a person begins to share their feelings we need to encourage them to continue without making them feel under undue pressure. In terms of what the listener should say, the best guideline is 'less is more.' The kind of response that can be helpful is:

• 'I'm so glad you're sharing this with me. Please go on.'
• 'You must have felt awful [or wonderful; or whatever is appropriate]. '
• 'Mmmmn,' or 'Uh uh,' at intervals, to show you're listening. Telling your partner that you'd really like to help, and asking if there is anything you can do, may also be appropriate.
• 'I can't really imagine what that must have felt like but I would like to try and understand. It would be good if you could explain in a bit more detail.'

By contrast, the types of responses that are decidedly unhelpful are:

• 'Well, it's silly to feel like that. You shouldn't have.'

- 'If you do such and such you'll feel better.'
- 'That reminds me of the time I felt just like that.'

This last response is particularly dangerous because it may appear that we want to demonstrate understanding and empathy. And we may well do so, but it shifts the focus from our partner's sharing to ourselves. It can be a helpful response if said in a slightly different form: 'That sounds a bit like how I felt once. Of course the situation may not be the same at all. Tell me more about ...'

If the feelings relate to a specific problem and you believe that you have a solution, it may not be helpful to offer the solution immediately. It might be better to say at a later time that you've got some thoughts about solving the problem and perhaps it would be helpful for you to share them. Jumping in with solutions too early, however well-intentioned, may actually make things worse.

Some people are sceptical about the value of even mentioning feelings, associating such discussion with clichés about therapy and psychiatry, which are often based more on comedy programmes than reality. However, such scepticism may only be an avoidance technique. Nevertheless, it is important to recognise we're not talking just about the importance of recognising feelings. Discussion about feelings may well need to lead to some kind of objective action.

Aids to effective communication

Many people would probably identify failure to communicate as the major reason for marriage breakdown. Most couples recognise the need for good communication but fail to make it happen. Sometimes, we can be either knowingly or unwittingly selfish. We can be too busy working out what we want to say next to be really listening to our partner. Or perhaps our partner is a very reflective thinker and needs time to respond. It is all too easy to hear a long silence, assume they have nothing to say and jump in with our next comment.

It is important to really listen to our partner when they are talking to us, and to:

- maintain lots of eye contact.
- reflect on what we think we have heard them say.
- wait until we are convinced we know what they mean before we put our point of view, or have our say.

Communicating love: the three types of love

To communicate love effectively to our partner, it is important that we are clear about what type of love we intend to communicate. In English we have only one word for love, but in Greek, the language in which the New Testament was written, there are several words for love. We can helpfully use three of these Greek words to distinguish between different types of love in marriage:

Eros

This is erotic or romantic love. The word itself isn't used in the New Testament because by the time of the New Testament writers, *eros* had come to have unacceptable associations in Greek culture. So the New Testament writers used other Greek words – principally, *epithumia* – to speak of physical attraction. However, we're using *eros* here as it is a much more familiar word.

Phileo

This is friendship love, intellectual attraction.

Agape

This love is very different from either *eros* or *phileo*. Whereas our *eros* or *phileo* love for someone is dependent on us finding them attractive in some way, *agape* is about choosing to love. It does not depend upon any sexual or intellectual attraction the other person might have for us. It is not an emotion, although emotions might accompany it. It is practical love, love in action, a love that keeps on giving against the odds. It is the love that God has for us and the love that is commanded by Jesus (see, for example, John 15:12). This is the love that will keep our marriage going through the tough times. If we cling to *agape* love when *eros* and *phileo* seem to have disappeared, then they can both be wonderfully restored, as many couples testify. *Agape* is the love that overcomes.

Communicating love: different languages

It is not enough in a marriage for us to assume that our partner knows we love them. They need to feel loved. Many communication and other problems can be tackled more easily, more successfully, when we are secure in feeling loved by our partner. We need to communicate love to one another. Not everyone has the same way of expressing and receiving love and it is important that we communicate love to our partner in a language that has real meaning for them. There are various different ways of communicating love.

Physical contact: for some people, touch is their natural language. Their way of communicating and receiving affection is through physical contact: hugs, cuddles and holding hands, to list a few. If you are naturally a physical person then you may assume that most other people are as well. For you, absence of physical contact probably suggests absence of love. But not all people are physical in this way and if your partner is not, then it is easy to misread the absence of physical contact.

Words: hearing the words 'I love you' tends to be more special for wives than for husbands, but if words are your partner's language of love then words of affection and appreciation are really important. The written word can be just as potent, possibly more so for some. Saying or writing such things as

'You're really special to me', 'I'm so proud of you', 'It's fun being married to you', can help to strengthen relationships, carrying them through difficult times. If this is your preferred way of communicating love then you will probably appreciate turning off the TV and just talking together. Conversation will be an important part of the relationship for you.

Helping: if this is your language, the person helping you doesn't necessarily need to be contributing a great deal to the task in hand. Just having them there, supporting you, encouraging you, contributing as much as they're able may be enough. If this doesn't come naturally to you, it may feel like just 'sitting around' and a waste of time. But it may not be; you may be communicating love very powerfully.

Giving and receiving gifts: in this way some people readily express affection, gratitude, esteem or caring. The gift does not have to be big or extravagant. Just a small token can mean a lot to someone if this is their language. Some husbands who have this language express their love by working hard to provide material things for their wives, perhaps working long hours. This can lead to problems if it is not the wife's way of receiving love. If she does not set much store by material wealth but simply enjoys their being together, then problems can arise.

Being together: for some people just being together in the same room or even just in the house is really important. If this is not your natural language, you may have some trouble accepting just how important it is to your partner. If it is their language, then however much you may tell them you love them, they might have trouble believing it if you are never around. They will not feel loved.

Virtually all of us do all of the above to some extent. The question here is how well we emphasise the one that is most important to our partner. It's rather like learning a foreign language. If we marry someone from our own culture then we'll generally understand one another pretty well, but if we marry someone from a different culture we need to learn each other's native language to maximise our chances of understanding everything about each other. For example, a husband buys his wife an expensive birthday gift because giving presents is his preferred way of communicating love. His wife's preferred way of receiving love is to spend time together. She would feel more loved with a less extravagant gift and her husband taking the day off to be with her. Of course the two things aren't mutually exclusive. If the couple are unaware of each other's preferred ways of giving and receiving love then in this instance the wife may not greet the gift with much enthusiasm, especially if her husband is late back from the office, and the husband will feel his love has been rejected. On the husband's birthday the mistake may be reversed: the wife plans, at great effort, a day out together whereas the husband was really hoping for a new set of golf clubs. In both cases what is intended as an expression of love may be received in a lukewarm way, perhaps leading to a sense of rejection.

Understanding different approaches to discussion and debate

In any relationship there will be important decisions to be made, issues to be discussed. We're thinking here about either issues that are in themselves important, such as where shall we spend Christmas, or should we buy a new car, or issues that are apparently trivial but have the potential to escalate into something serious. In general we have differing styles when it comes to approaching discussion. There are three natural approaches, each with advantages but also serious disadvantages. Two of these have distinct advantages that need to be learnt. In what follows, the original research has been simplified as we're focusing on the ways the principles relate to marriage.

Rapid Verbaliser

Such people are energised by discussion. They approach any issue or discussion with great vigour. They readily verbalise the points they want to make. They quickly muster arguments in support of their position. The more heated the debate, the more they respond. They may have the attitude and mindset of a winner, wanting to 'get the last word' against all odds. The winning may become an end in itself, regardless of what the discussion is about.

Possible advantages: usually able to tackle issues. Able to confront.

Possible disadvantages: may say hurtful, unfair, unkind things, even when they are not meant or relevant in order to win. May turn trivial debates into major conflicts. Will probably feel bad about themself at the end of the discussion, even if having a perception of having won. Will feel worse if defeated. Will feel guilty about the things said to partner. Partner may feel angry or resentful about things said. Issues may never be settled.

Reflective Thinker

These people generally need time to reflect on what they want to say before they are comfortable verbalising their thoughts. They find rapid dialogue unhelpful, possibly disempowering. The more heated the discussion or debate becomes, the more uncomfortable they feel. They withdraw, either figuratively by becoming more and more silent, or literally, by turning away, standing up and turning their back on the other person; even physically leaving the room.

Possible advantages: will give serious consideration to issues; will not be side-tracked by a desire to win. Will usually be prepared to tackle issues when they are presented quietly and thoughtfully. May be more comfortable with written analysis of issues.

Possible disadvantages: may be so disempowered by the process that no discussion is possible. If other participant in the discussion become heated, they may withdraw completely. Issues needing to be tackled may never be addressed. Partner will probably feel frustrated that things are never tackled. Tension levels within the relationship will rise.

A rare, but very real, problem may be one where the reflective thinker has real difficulty verbalising statements and arguments, and is therefore unable to express their feelings. Frustration may build up to such an extent that the next time their partner, or anyone else, confronts them they may lash out verbally or physically, sometimes with a degree of violence. This potential problem is more common in men than women and wives need to be particularly sensitive to husbands who are normally quiet and gentle but who explode in temper from time to time. It is easy to see the problem as the fault of the partner who has erupted, when it should be seen as a joint problem to be faced and overcome together. (This is not to be confused with systematic, ongoing, violence from one partner to another, which is a more serious matter.)

Yielder – someone who gives in

Yielders will avoid being drawn into any kind of debate. They may say things without reflecting on the issues, such as: 'I'm sure you've thought about this'; 'go ahead and do whatever you want'; 'I don't have an opinion'; 'I don't want to think about that'; 'I'm not interested in that', or the classic: 'I don't mind' even when the issue is important and they ought to be participating in any discussion or debate.

Possible advantages: may be genuinely easy-going and have few strong opinions. May want to encourage the partner to take the lead. Less liable to get upset over trivial issues.

Possible disadvantages: will place a lot of responsibility on the partner. May opt out of the decision-making process, then criticise decision. May not be concerned enough about the relationship to want to make the effort. May acquiesce for a number of times then decide it's their turn to have their way about an issue, even if that is unreasonable. May agree to do things the partner's way, or may say nothing at all, then go off and do things the way they want.

The above three approaches generally cover most people's initial approach to debate and especially conflict situations. Each can move on to the next category, which is a marked improvement for effective communication in the relationship.

Compromiser

They try to find an equitable or middle position for solving issues. They approach issues with a negotiation technique, expecting to get something out of the negotiation but recognising that their partner will get something too.

Possible advantages: prepared to take partner's point of view into account. Capable of moving issues forward in a way that is comfortable, even if not entirely satisfying, for all parties.

Possible disadvantages: may be mildly selfish, prepared to give way on some things of secondary concern, in order to get their own way with things of priority concern. May not recognise that in some situations, compromise is just not possible.

The best way of handling disagreements is to work to a resolution; with one person, but ideally both partners, being a resolver.

Resolver

They want any issue to be dealt with in the best possible way for everyone involved. They are genuinely concerned for the well-being of their partner and for the good of the relationship. They approach the issue in a gentle and non-threatening way. They take time to listen to their partner and reflect back to them what they think they have heard, in order to be sure they really understand the other point of view. They are open about their feelings on the issue and thus are prepared to makes themselves vulnerable.

Advantages: this is the best of all styles of approaching issues. It ensures that our partner feels that their thoughts and feelings are valued. It will enable difficult issues to be dealt with calmly and non-confrontationally and therefore reduces the risk of conflict. It is possible for everyone to feel good at the end of the process and for important issues to be settled.

Disadvantages: it takes time and effort to be a good resolver. The discussion is slowed down and the process will probably need to have a block of quality time allocated to it in order to reach a satisfactory conclusion. However, the more couples practise resolution the quicker the process becomes. It's rather like learning to ballroom dance. At first it is difficult to take complementary steps that will get you round the dance floor. You may tread on each other's toes or stumble. But after practice, the dancing becomes increasingly elegant and appears almost effortless.

As we've implied above, it's hardly necessary to go through a complex resolution discussion for every decision of married life! The answer to the question 'What do you want for breakfast?' genuinely may be 'I don't mind.'

Combinations

Ardent verbaliser and reflective thinker

An ardent verbaliser (or 'winner') married to a reflective thinker, (or 'withdrawer') may describe the withdrawer as sulking, unwilling to face issues, never wanting to communicate. They may say things such as 'I'm the only one who makes an effort in this relationship', 'Why do you always run away from discussions?' or 'Why can't you face up to issues?' The more frustrated and loudly verbal they become, the less willing their partner will be to discuss issues. Winners have been known to chase withdrawers from room to room to get a good fight out of them!

A withdrawer may describe a winner as loud, unreasonable, never prepared to listen to anyone else's point of view, aggressive, angry. Each can easily become increasingly frustrated with the other and therefore important issues may not get discussed.

Ardent verbaliser and yielder

Ardent verbalisers may appear always to get their own way and debate may be short, perhaps frustratingly short. One real danger for the relationship is that the yielder may give in or appear to give in, go off and do things their own way regardless of what was discussed. This can lead to a lack of trust and hurt.

Ardent verbaliser and ardent verbaliser

Two winners may have some explosive encounters. If both are energised by conflict they may also have some spectacular reconciliation scenes; however, the damage they can do to one another is potentially great. Each may say whatever hurtful things they can think of, in order to win. There may be a great deal of hurt for each to forgive and to be healed from.

Reflective thinker and reflective thinker

Two reflective thinkers may have a very quiet marriage in terms of disagreements but each may be secretly frustrated about issues that never get aired or dealt with.

Considerate Debate

There will always be issues in any relationship that need dealing with. Many of them are relatively trivial and can be discussed and resolved amicably without recourse to any sophisticated communication techniques. But there are inevitably some issues that have an emotional element for one or both partners. These issues are the ones that need careful handling if they are not to degenerate into conflicts, arguments or rows.

How to discuss emotive issues

- Try not to discuss difficult issues when emotions are at their height. This may be the time to listen to each other's feelings instead. If it's important enough to get all steamed up about then it's important enough to set time aside to discuss analytically, even in a busy life. If it's not that important, don't allow yourself to become irritated by the issue.
- Agree an appropriate time to discuss the issue, ideally when there are no external pressures.
- Take time to pray about it beforehand.
- Be relaxed. Some people, especially if they are ardent verbalisers, find it helpful to imagine putting down an imaginary weapon.
- Make yourself vulnerable. Own up to your feelings. Talk in 'I' statements rather than 'you' statements which focus on your partner's perceived, or even real, mistakes. Saying: 'I feel so angry with you because ...' is not a helpful way to begin!
- Talk in terms of your partner's behaviour, not character. In Parliament one MP is not permitted to call another MP a liar. If they do they can be temporarily excluded from the House. What they can say is 'The honourable gentleman (or lady) has misled the house.' The first is an attack on character, the second a statement about behaviour.

Steps to make a conflict constructive rather than destructive

- Alert your partner to the fact that there is a problem. 'I have a problem I think you can help me with' is a phrase that many couples have found helpful. If this becomes a bit of a joke, so much the better. To move the conflict onto a humorous level at the start can be helpful – providing the humour is mutual!
- Be gentle in the way you bring the problem to your partner's attention. Use non-threatening language while ensuring that you have clearly communicated the problem.
- Be honest about your needs and concerns. Explain the related feelings rather than arguing the objective facts.

• Don't be too 'heavy' in your communication. Lighten up, joke if possible, smile. Recognise that neither of you is perfect. You both have little habits and foibles which can seriously irritate your partner. We are all on a journey to become what our Heavenly Father wants us to be: more and more like Christ. God intends our partners to help and support us on this journey.

Questions

1. Think about disagreements you have in your marriage. Are there common themes or patterns which may offer some insight into changes you might need to make?

2. Think about how you approach discussion, joint decision-making and conflict situations. Of the categories given above, which one do you think is most like you? Which one is most like your partner? What can you do to become a resolver?

3. Are there any issues that you believe ought to be discussed in your marriage but you've both been avoiding because they are too emotive? What do you think are the risks of continuing to avoid these issues?

4. With regard to everyday matters, what things does your partner do that annoy you intensely or make you angry, perhaps out of all proportion? Does your partner know why you react in this way? Do you know why? If possible, think about what you can both do to develop better understanding.

5. Do you find it easier to communicate criticism rather than encouragement? Think about how you can communicate more encouragement and less criticism.

Gender in Marriage – it's not Just Biology!

Points to ponder

Before thinking about gender issues in detail you might like to think about some questions, and then review your answers having read the chapter.

1. *What do you think are the problems about having a discussion about gender issues in the church?*
2. *Do you find the Bible's teaching about the role of wives difficult or unpalatable?*
3. *How would you defend what the Bible says about the relationship between husbands and wives to a non-Christian feminist?*
4. *What do you think are the most important points about the relationship between husbands and wives in the Biblical teaching on marriage?*
5. *What things infuriate you about members of the opposite sex? [Don't take this one too seriously!]*

Danger! Unexploded mines!

To have a debate about gender issues can feel like walking through a minefield. We know it can be done but every step is taken hesitantly on tiptoe and we anticipate an explosion at any moment. Throughout the Western world, much of twentieth-century history has included confrontation regarding the role of women: the Suffragettes and the campaign for votes for women in Edwardian Britain; the first exclusion of women from the war effort in Nazi Germany, except as child bearers until Goebbel's 'Total War' speech that radically altered German thinking; the Women's Liberation movement associated initially with 60s' America. Less spectacular, but of great importance, was a shift in the role of women in society, including women taking on jobs and careers that were previously considered 'male only' professions and equal pay for equal work. It's not so long ago that an employer could pay a woman less than a man for doing the same job. Like many major shifts in society, the change has often resembled a war rather than a debate, typified by battle lines being firmly drawn up and positions voiced in extreme terms. The church has not been isolated from these issues. For many churches the change over recent years has been relatively spectacular, most notably with the ordination of women and women preaching in non-conformist churches. Even churches that have vigorously resisted any such change have been affected. Whereas even half a century ago their position would have been taken as the assumed norm, they now have had to justify their stance and defend it against attack, not only from without but also from within.

Because of the emotive nature of the topic, genuine debate on gender issues in churches has become risky and therefore rare. By default it has become something of a no-go area. Teaching and discussion are often hesitant and limited or typified by dogmatism. The intention of this chapter is not to advocate a particular line but to encourage people to think through how gender issues impact on their own lives and relationships, particularly in many areas of marriage. If we are to live out what the Bible has to teach us about the importance of gender differences in marriage, it is vital that we think about the topic without drawing up battle lines.

Gender differences: anecdotal or scientific?

One of the blocks to couples living as one in the way that God intends may be that the husband and wife have an incomplete understanding of how gender differences impact on them. We want to make it clear that we are in no way suggesting that all men exhibit what could be described as 'masculine' behaviour, nor do all women behave in an exclusively 'feminine' manner. It would be very wrong to stereotype people in terms of gender. What we can legitimately do is identify patterns that are gender based. There will always be exceptions to the pattern but these neither make a person less masculine or feminine. The fact remains that from the time we were in the womb, powerful hormones were at work defining some of us as male, with masculine characteristics, and some as female, with feminine characteristics. This is dependent upon whether we have x:y chromosomes, or x:x chromosomes. These differences do go beyond the ones that are visible. The Bible has always claimed that men and women are different, and this is being increasingly recognised by the scientific community as true.

Back in the 60s and 70s gender was a dangerous subject. To suggest that there were any differences between men and women – other than a few bits of plumbing and décor associated with procreation – was to make yourself the target of the Women's Lib movement. Scientists and other researchers into gender differences have struggled for a long time to try and differentiate the real, physiological differences between men and women from those which are due to cultural and environmental influences. Recently, hi-tech developments have made it possible to show that there are radical differences in the way that some men and women process information.

A research project used equipment to 'photograph' what was happening in the brains of a group of people while they were thinking. An equal number of men and women were given pairs of nonsense words and told to work out if the words rhymed. The reason was that this would ensure that it was the processing of information that was being recorded, not memory or recall. What the researchers found was that for all the men taking part in the experiment brain activity occurred only in the left hemisphere. In the majority of the women, areas in both hemispheres of their brains were active while processing was taking place.[1] It would be dangerous and unscientific to push conclusions from this experiment too far, but this evidence may in time become a basis for providing explanations for other differences. For instance, many women multi-task, to a greater or lesser degree of efficiency. It has been found in training at high speed of pilots of jet aircraft, women are better at a multi-tasking exercise than the men. Conversely, men tend to be better at single-focusing. Men are able to 'lose' themselves in a project or interest. Wives sometimes accuse husbands of putting work, the computer, sport or other interests at the top of a priority list. The truth is that men don't think in that way. At any one time they will have a priority list of one, and when something has their attention it is likely to have their entire attention. These differences may also explain why many men find it difficult to have an emotional discussion, or sometimes even to access their emotions. The right hemisphere of the brain is the one which appears to have most to do with processing emotion, and this is the side which was not active in any of the males who were involved in the experiment involving information processing. Again, we wish to emphasise that we are speaking in generalisations, not of stereotypes. There are undoubtedly men who do not find emotional discussion difficult, and women who do, but many men need to approach an emotional discussion via an analytical dialogue. Generally, men find an emotional discussion disturbing and extremely difficult. Many women use part of the right brain to process information automatically, so for them a discussion involving emotions will come more easily. In fact, many women need to talk about issues when they have had a row or disagreement. For them, closure after an argument may be hugely difficult unless they are able to talk about it. Men, on the other hand, usually find talking about a row or issue disturbing. They will often say such things to their wives as 'Why can't you just draw a line under that?', 'It's in the past, things are different now', 'Talking

[1] Shaywitz, *et al*. 'Sex Differences in the functional organisation of the brain for language.' *Nature*, number 373 pp. 607–609

about it will just bring it all back and make you feel worse.' A husband may feel frustrated when his wife wants to talk about something that has happened earlier because he feels that he can't do anything about it. He doesn't realise that just by listening he is helping his wife to get over whatever the problem had been. This process can be much smoother if a wife can say things such as: 'I need you to listen to this. I know you can't do anything about it but just telling you will be helpful for me', BEFORE launching into whatever is on her mind. Other helpful preambles are such phrases as 'I need to talk about this. I'm not blaming you, it's not your fault but talking about it to you would really help.' If the incident is something the husband has done then a phrase such as ' I know you didn't mean to hurt me, and I do forgive you, but I was upset and I need to tell you how I feel so that I can really get over it.' Wives also generally need to get things sorted out before they are going to feel like making love. Another difference which may seem trivial but which sometimes leads to minor, or even major, dissents is that nearly all men are unable to see an object in a cupboard or the refrigerator, when it's behind something else!

Gender differences: some Old Testament data

The Bible has quite a bit to say about the similarities and the differences between men and women. Genesis 1 emphasises our similarities whereas Genesis 2 highlights something of the differences between men and women. It makes no difference for the purposes of this discussion whether we regard these accounts as literal historical truth or poetic truth. The fact is that they are true in some way, which God wants us to take seriously.

Genesis 1:27 tells us that God created men and women in his image; equal, but different. They were given the same status and the same task, to subdue to the earth and rule over it. They were to work at this together, in harmony. Most husbands and wives find working together on a project in harmony, under God, is a rewarding and joyful experience. However, some of the subtleties of Genesis 2:7 are not obvious in English. The Hebrew contains some wordplays: for example the name Adam is very closely related to the word for ground. Indeed 'ground' doesn't convey all the nuances of the Hebrew. It can be understood in a variety of ways but the picture is probably red clay. The verb used here of God's creative act is not the same word as used in the first chapter which is best understood as 'create' (Hebrew *bara*). Here the verb used is *yatsar*. This verb can be translated as 'form' or 'fashion'. However, it is associated with the idea of a potter moulding clay, forming it according to his will. The image is of God forming the first human being from fresh clay. The potential is limited only by the skill of the potter. And since here the craftsman is God Himself, then … well, we are left to draw our own conclusions. What appears at first reading to be a simple report of God making Adam, in reality conveys some important truths that have relevance for marriage. Clay has two states. Before it is fired it is soft, malleable, easily moulded. God is in the process of transforming the clay into something that pleases him. At this point it is good to remember that only the potter has the right to mould the clay; wives may think that the potter needs a hand, and indeed God does sometimes use close relationships in this process, but He is the only one who has a right to decide this. It is not acceptable for wives to indulge in a bit of 'improving' on their own account! Clay also has another state. When it is fired it is capable of having many vital uses. Clay vessels have an intrinsic grace and beauty but they are generally something useful, or functional. Certainly, this was true of pottery in early civilisations, when grain, oil, wine and water were all stored in clay vessels. The Dead Sea scrolls were kept safe in stone jars in a hillside cave for approximately two thousand years. Since their discovery and removal from the jars they now are kept in thermostatically controlled, air-conditioned sterile conditions. This image speaks to us of man's basic nature. Generally, most men gain a great deal from what they do. The things that involve them – their jobs, professions, sports, hobbies – give them a great deal of satisfaction.

Although clay is very strong when fired, capable of holding many gallons of water or measures of grain, it is also brittle and therefore easily broken. Wives would do well to be aware of this. Husbands, however strong they may seem, can be broken by harsh words, criticism, unfeeling or unthinking comments.

In Genesis 2:18 God says that it is not good for the man to be alone. Adam has a perfect relationship with God, yet something is still lacking in his life. God says that He will make what is often translated as a 'helper' for Adam. In English this word is far too weak to convey the type of person God was about to create. The Hebrew term (*'ezer kenegdo*) is not easy to translate with a single word. It is a term that doesn't mean subservient but someone who stands alongside, or acts as a counterpart; someone who intervenes on behalf of another. It's a strong term, one associated with the military: an adjutant to a general. Although it is not identical in meaning, the term has close similarities with the New Testament word *paracletos*, the word Jesus uses in John to describe the role of the Holy Spirit. To use the imagery of the modern business world, traditionally the idea of 'helper' has invoked the idea of a subservient personal assistant whereas the actual idea is much more akin to that of lawyer.

In verses 21 and 22 of Genesis 2 we read how God put Adam into a deep sleep and removed one of his ribs. From this He created Eve. The way Eve was made, being taken from another person, is a powerful reminder of how much satisfaction most women find in relationships. However much of a career person a woman may be, however successful at what she does, the relationships formed at work and home will be of great importance to her. Research shows that single women are much better at forming networks and relationships than single men. This is perhaps most obvious with bereavement. Widowers often find it much harder to cope than widows. The word used to describe God creating Eve is very different to the one used for Adam. The Hebrew verb (*banah*) literally means to build, or construct. Hardly a flattering term at first sight! But the idea it conveys is crucial to a Biblical understanding of women. What we are presented with at the very outset is a word appropriate for the material with which God chooses to work. Whereas He moulded man from the malleable clay, the image here is along the lines of Him chiselling Eve out of a strong, resistant material: Adam's rib. This is a clue to the nature of women; they are created with great inner strength. This strength is not about personality, but inner character. Many women have quiet, gentle personalities but this does not alter the fact that they were created to withstand much. Pregnancy and childbirth are an obvious example. There is an old joke that if men were responsible for childbirth no family would have more than one child. The Bible has many examples of strong women. Naomi must have been a gentle person to have generated such love from Ruth, but she was tough enough to survive great loss and face the arduous and bitter return to her native land (see Ruth chapter 1). 1 Samuel 25 gives us a great example of the principle we have come across in Genesis 2. While still on the run from Saul, David and his followers request the assistance of Nabal. The text clearly presents Nabal as an unpleasant fellow, and he not only rejects David's request but ridicules him. David is furious and plans over-the-top revenge. Meanwhile Abigail, Nabal's wife, hears of her husband's inappropriate behaviour and goes on his behalf to intercede with David. She approaches David with gentleness and tact oozing from every pore, yet it must have taken a great deal of courage and inner strength to plead for her husband in such a way. David listens to her and blesses her for her discernment.

Gender differences: some New Testament data

The passages about the role of husbands and wives that prompt the most heated debate are found in the New Testament. We do not intend to discuss every aspect of such passages here but to do two related things: firstly, demonstrate that we can take out much of the heat from such passages without compromising the authority of Scripture; and secondly, think about how these passages are really relevant for our marriages.

The moment we read Scripture we interpret it. We may talk, or hear others talk, about the plain meaning of Scripture but strictly speaking there can be no such thing. We read through our own cultural spectacles. This is true for anything we read or see. Have you ever read jokes from foreign magazines? Even if we understand the words, the jokes usually don't work for us at all. Humour is more than just understanding the words, it's also about understanding the cultural background. Another example is when we look at art from a non-Western culture. We may appreciate it or even like it, but are we sure we understand it? We are less aware of these cultural differences in our generation not primarily because we live in the so-called global village but because the global village is dominated by Western culture.

Language alone is not the root issue. If a British person reads American literature they may well be able to enjoy and appreciate the novel. But if they examine their attitude as they read they will do so as something of a spectator rather than participant. Some things will be clear but also alien. If they have been to the United States and know a lot about American culture from the media, the explanatory insights will be learnt rather than part of native upbringing. When we read of someone driving in an American novel, most British readers have to make a conscious effort to imagine the driver in the left-hand seat. Similarly, when we visit most countries we have to make a conscious effort to look right-left-right rather than the left-right-left that became ingrained in us as children.

The New Testament is not a product of Western culture. We know this in theory but modern translations, helpful though they are, obscure this obvious truth. Plus we probably want to say that it is relevant to all people of all times, including Western culture. The reality is that we usually read the New Testament unaware that we are doing so wearing modern Western spectacles. To be able to read it in the original Greek, of course, helps us to put our spectacles to one side but even that is not enough. It's another example of reading the words as a spectator. Only by trying to get into the culture and mindset of a first-century Mediterranean reader will we start really to develop an understanding of what the text means. The good news is that in one sense this is easier than learning Greek, and providing we read a good translation, remembering that it is only a translation, then we can get a long way.

But what's all this got to do with gender? Quite a lot. Paul and other New Testament writers are perhaps most misunderstood by lay readers when dealing with gender issues. There are two opposite pitfalls which we must do our best to avoid if we are to understand and apply what they have to say to our everyday lives. The first pitfall is that we write off what they have to say because it seems so far removed from our culture and experience of life in the West in the twenty-first century. But while the background to their words may be far removed, the principles remain relevant. The trick is to spot the principles. The second pitfall is to try to insist on a literal application of what the words say. The problem here is another, far more dangerous and subjective form of interpretation. When we read through the New Testament we don't take all of it literally. We recognise, not so much through deep theology but common sense, that some of it is obviously not meant literally. When Jesus talks about us cutting off our hands or plucking out our eyes if they offend us we recognise that He is using Middle Eastern hyperbole (Matthew 18:8,9). And many churches that are committed to the authority of the Bible are quite content to interpret Paul's injunction to greet one another with a holy kiss as a handshake or hug, which is more comfortable in our society. If we claim to take the Bible literally then we shall either have to learn to come to terms with getting by with one hand and one eye or accept that we are hypocrites. The moment we decide what should and shouldn't be taken literally we interpret. And when we interpret we do so from a cultural perspective.

One helpful way of approaching some of the Pauline passages is to recognise that Paul often uses a common rabbinic model for his arguments: outlining a theological principle and then supporting it with points of application. We can witness this in Colossians 3:1–4:1.

Colossians 3:1–17 is all about theological truths (the *why*) and lifestyle principles (the *what*). But there is scant help from Paul in these first 17 verses on specific application (the *how*). However, chapter 3:18–4:1 is about how to implement the why and what of verses 1–17. Three twinned relationships are cited: husbands and wives; children and fathers; slaves and masters. Instead of presenting us with detailed lifestyle blueprints for each role, Paul give us warnings about particular pitfalls into which these people can commonly fall. But neither party is given additional scope because of the others' Christian obedience. Children have a tendency to be disobedient; even the best fathers can occasionally abuse their authority. Slaves – we might extend this to people in badly paid jobs – have a tendency to work harder when the boss is watching. Masters can slip into treating their slaves with less than perfect justice and consideration. But we are unlikely to mistake these brief comments for a complete summary of the relationships. We can understand verses 18 and 19 in the same way. On a common-sense level most of us easily recognise that wives find being subject doesn't always comes naturally because women are strong, not weak! And husbands can find it all too easy to be unloving and bitter when problems arise. Such an approach allows us to view the theological principles of 3:1–17 as non-negotiables but 3:18–4:1 as application, almost, without under-estimating the importance of the verses, seeing them as inspired 'helpful hints'. Application may not be non-negotiable but it may require understanding and perhaps even reinterpreting with regard to culture. Which is, of course, what most of us do with chapter 4 verse 3.

Ephesians 5:22–33 is perhaps the best known of the relevant passages related to marriage. But reading it against the principle of verse 21, where Paul tells us to submit ourselves to one another, prevents inappropriate chauvinism. Husbands are to show love; wives respect. We can easily acknowledge that Paul has a lot of theological points to make about marriage but he also has helpful things to say, things which make excellent sense in psychological terms. Sadly, these things all too often have been misinterpreted over the years. If we are to have a Biblical understanding of marriage and aim to live out Biblical marriage principles then we need to reclaim the practical truth that Paul offers us. And when we do we find it liberating, not restricting. In Ephesians 5:22 wives are told to submit themselves to their husbands. (Assuming this is exactly what the verse means! In fact the verb is lacking although it is implied on the basis of verse 21.) Over the centuries this verse, perhaps more than any other, has been regularly misused in our society; it is almost guaranteed to make wives see red! In some cultures it has been seized upon by husbands with glee, and used as a carte blanche for repressive behaviour. But of course the verse is not addressed to husbands! It is addressed to wives: women whom God made from tough material, women who have a tremendous inner strength. And that inner strength is capable of being misused, directed in harsh ways against our husbands. It can tear relationships apart. This does not mean wives should be constantly overridden, or have their wishes ignored. Far from it: they were given this strength by God Himself. But there are ways of using that strength to make both husband and wife stronger and the relationship more secure. If a wife knows that this verse applies to her personally and she is guilty of nagging, criticising, or even bullying her husband, then it may be a challenge. However, displaying patience, gentleness and humour in the face of inexplicable behaviour should mean an untroubled understanding of this verse.

In verse 25 Paul tells husbands to love their wives as Christ loved the church, and gave Himself up for her. Its familiarity should not cause us to overlook how sensational Paul's comments are. Here is Paul the Rabbi, steeped in Jewish tradition and the Torah, talking about the relationship between a husband and wife. In his tradition we might expect him to say something like 'Husbands, esteem your wives,' or 'Husbands, value your wives as mothers of your children.' But no, he says 'Love'! In our culture, where the word love is bandied about freely and where marriages are made, not arranged, we might miss the impact of this statement. The first-century readers of this statement would have been bowled over with surprise. 'What, Paul? *Love*? Do you really *mean* love?' And not the more common *phileo*, friendship love, but *agape*, a relatively obscure Greek word seized on by the New Testament writers to convey the idea of the love God has for us and the love we should have for one another: a very practical love, the longsuffering, giving love that God displays to us. And why is Paul giving this unlikely command? Because he knows that it is what wives need. Not what they deserve, some of the time, but what they need. They need to *feel* at the centre of the husband's life, above the rest of the family, above sport, above career, job, interests; even, in this day and age, above computers. Relationships are hugely important and women often struggle with feelings of low self-esteem. Wives do not feel able to take it for granted that they are loved; they need to be reassured. Taxing for husbands, sometimes challenging, when wives are being crabby or unreasonable, but part of the ingredient of a successful marriage.

In verse 33 wives are told to respect their husbands. This is what husbands need. It does not matter how much respect they get at work, with peers or friends: if they come home and are constantly belittled, moaned at or criticised, they will not feel loved by their wives, however much they are told that they are loved. Men have fragile egos; they are created from brittle material, easily broken. The hurt inflicted is often disguised under a sullen response, an angry retort, or a withdrawal, which may be interpreted as sulking.

1 Peter 3:1–7 is another important passage about marriage and one that appears remarkably chauvinist. We've talked above about the importance of a literal interpretation of Scripture being also consistent. We're not trying to dissuade anyone who believes that these verses should be applied literally and at face value. But many Christians who are committed to the authority of Scripture will have difficulty with taking these verses at face value. The temptation is to put the passage, or parts of it, to one side. So how can we apply this passage in marriage without taking it at face value but without compromising the authority of

Scripture? As with many Biblical passages it is important to identify the root principle rather than the expression of the principle. In order to understand what the passage is really about it is vital to understand the Roman cultural background plus some allusions from the Old Testament, which would have been obvious to the Jewish hearers and readers but may escape us. We can note several points:

1. In the ancient world, wives and women generally had virtually no legal rights, including no automatic right of inheritance. The rights given to women in the Jewish law were a stunning exception. In this sense wives were very much the weaker sex, dependent on their husbands. No doubt many wives found informal ways to influence their husbands, but that is another story! However, Peter urges husbands to regard their wives as fellow heirs under the new covenant, something we might take for granted as we read it, but amazingly liberating for that time. The joint equality before God is foundational in the passage but easy for us to overlook.

2. The bulk of the advice here is addressed to wives. This is logical. A non-Christian wife of a Christian husband would have been expected to conform to his lifestyle and go to church with him. Conversion itself would be expected of her (see, for example, Acts 16:33). But the Christian wife of a non-Christian husband could exert no such pressure. Her witness had to be lifestyle; even open debate about evangelistic topics could have been considered unacceptable and disloyal.

3. Well-to-do women had a lot of time at their disposal. References in ancient writers to how such women spent their time on matters of personal appearance are not uncommon. We mustn't forget how long hairdressing and application of cosmetics would have taken in the ancient world; much longer than with today's equivalents. To be perfectly coiffured and well made-up would have been a status symbol, a way of demonstrating financial and social status.

4. Even in the Old Testament we come across criticism of women who enjoy flaunting their appearance in such ways. They are identified by the prophets as specific targets for God's judgement. For example: Isaiah 3:16–22 and Amos 4:1–3. Sarah, Abraham's wife, is cited in direct contrast to such women. Her commitment to her husband was in practice commitment to the covenant God made with Abraham (Genesis 12:1–3), which we may note was made with her husband and not directly with her. Her obedience was the vehicle for the foundation of the Jewish race. Now most men cannot really imagine the pain of childbirth. But can even a mother imagine the pain of being pregnant and giving birth in one's nineties as Sarah did (Genesis 17:17)? No wonder Isaiah 51:2 talks of Sarah's pain.

So how do these points relate to the present day? If we are to apply the principles in this passage, our challenge is to be clear about the outworking of these principles in our society. Common sense and consideration of the background to the passage strongly suggests that Peter is not condemning women for wearing lipstick and some jewellery! The question is really about a wife's priorities. Perhaps a modern equivalent to the behaviour Peter warns against is the wife who spends hours every week at a health club, weekly visits to hairdressers, specialist nail shops and frequent shopping trips to buy unnecessary designer clothes. We're not implying these things are bad in moderation but inappropriate for a Christian when they dominate life. By contrast, one hallmark of a Christian wife is to be one who, like Sarah, is committed to seeing things through with her husband, even when circumstances are tough: not a wife who stands back from her husband and leaves him to struggle with difficult circumstances alone. There is also a special encouragement here for the Christian wife married to a non-Christian husband: an encouragement to witness with her lifestyle. We know of one woman who became a Christian long after her marriage; she and her husband had several children. Her response after conversion was to spend long

hours reading her Bible and praying. Her family felt she was
neglecting them. After praying about the situation she felt it
right to seriously reduce the time she spent on prayer and Bible
reading. This spoke to her family, whereas her explicit evange-
lism had fallen on deaf ears. They began showing an interest
in her new-found belief and eventually all came to know Christ
for themselves. She and her husband now have a flourishing
Christian ministry.

Modern husbands too should find the passage relevant for
them. Without getting into the whole issue of equal rights
Christian husbands can have opportunities to apply the principles Peter raises here. No matter how much of a career a wife
may have, she is still subject to expectations from those around
her. If a house is untidy or unclean, it tends to be the wife, not the
husband, who is judged by others. A recent study has shown
that while couples may claim to share the housework equally, in
reality working wives do over four times as much as working
husbands. While there may be a challenge in this to audit actual
time devoted to housework, the more obvious challenge from
this passage is that the husband should be sensitive to the reali-
ties of modern life and make an effort to understand how they
impact on his wife. Another example may be the wife who is
criticised by others because she chooses not to juggle mother-
hood and paid employment but stays home with the children,
even if this results in the family struggling financially. Again
there will be opportunities for the husband to demonstrate
understanding and support.

Before leaving this passage we need to note one more thing.
Theological truth has an important psychological dimension.
The truth here can banish deep-seated fears common in
marriage. Genuinely lived out, this passage reassures the wife
that her husband's love isn't based on the beauty of her youth
and the husband that his wife's respect is not conditional on his
achievements. The wife who is confident that her husband
won't be tempted to trade her in for a younger model can
feel secure in the marriage and blossom. The husband who
is confident that his wife will not ridicule him, especially in

public, even when he has done something stupid, can feel loved, supported and upheld.

One theme that comes across in these passages is that, just as God gives us what we need rather than what we deserve, so we should give to our partner what they need rather than what they deserve. A husband may feel justified in withholding love until he feels his wife is worthy of it; a wife may feel justified in withholding respect for her husband until he has earned it. But such perspectives are unbiblical. Love is to be given even when the wife is at her most unlovable just as Christ did to the church; respect is to be given even when the husband is at his most contemptible. If such love and respect are given rather than withheld then we may well find that the wife becomes much more worthy of love and the husband worthy of respect. The result comes from the giving.

Questions

1. Think back to your wedding day. What were your aims about the type of husband/wife you were intending to be? How have those intentions changed?

2. (a) For husbands:
   How close are you to loving your wife as Christ loved the church? What is stopping you loving your wife as Christ loved the church? What can you do to overcome the obstacles?
   (b) For wives:
   On a scale of 1–10, how good are you at respecting your husband? How can you communicate more respect to your husband in private; in front of family members; in public?

3. What causes you to criticise your partner? In what ways can you support your partner more and criticise them less?

4. (a) For husbands:
   What can you do to help your wife appreciate that she is not
   at the bottom of your list of priorities?
   (b) For wives:
   In what ways would it be good to pay more attention to your
   husband?

5. Are there things about your partner that you now think of
   as annoying habits that you used to think were endearing
   features? Are there gender differences that you need to learn
   to laugh at together?

6. If a stranger was to watch a video replay of your last week,
   what would they conclude about your priorities?

Who am I? Who are You?

This topic tends to generate one of two reactions. For some, it is the core issue that gets to the very heart of their own marriage, giving them key insights into understanding why certain difficulties keep arising. By contrast, some individuals find it helpful in theory but not especially relevant to their own marriage situation. If, after reading the chapter, your reaction is the former, then give yourself time and space to consider and pray about the issues. If your reaction is the latter, don't feel you should look for problems that may not be there.

The impact of past experiences on the present

In the first chapter we thought about how childhood expectations about marriage impact on our adult views. We now turn to consider the impact of past experiences; the accumulation of a whole host of experiences from earliest childhood onwards. Past experiences contribute, whether we know it or not, to the person that we are today.

None of us come into marriage newly hatched. Regardless of how young or how old we were when we married, we will have had diverse experiences which contribute to our identity; how we perceive ourselves and how others see us. These experiences include family background and upbringing, education, peer groups, culture and so on. In colloquial terms we can describe many of these things as 'emotional baggage', some of which may be good and helpful, some damaging and unhelpful and some a mix of good and bad, helpful and unhelpful. Anyone who has had anything to do with counselling, even if only from a distance, will know that counsellors, therapists and psychiatrists frequently encourage clients to examine their childhood. This can prompt some sceptics to dismiss counselling activity as being too concerned with the past rather than the present. The truth is past experiences impact on the present in ways which we cannot avoid just by pooh-poohing the history. Maybe the impact is a conscious one, but often the impact will be on a subconscious level, so we won't always notice what is happening.

Before we go any further you might like to try this simple three-part exercise

1. *Make yourself as physically comfortable as possible and, after you've finished reading these instructions, close your eyes. Think back to a childhood experience that made you very happy. Spend a minute or so reliving the experience in your memory. When you've finished, open your eyes and go on to the next part of the exercise.*
2. *Next, do the same thing but this time recall an experience that made you very unhappy, perhaps even frightened you.*
3. *Now try and take a mental pace back and review your present feelings while you were thinking of these two past experiences. Probably you didn't just remember the feelings but, to some extent, relived them while remembering the past event. You would not have been under any illusion that the events were not in the past but their impact may well have continued to the present via feelings.*

Now this is a simple exercise, and it is unlikely that the present feelings will have been very powerful; but for them to exist even to a low degree highlights the principle that although an event may be in the past, the emotions and feelings associated with that event may continue into the present.

If the childhood experience was very powerful at the time, the more likely it is that the associated emotions and feelings will affect us now. We can think of an experience being powerful in one of two ways. Firstly, it may be a single event that was particularly striking: being involved in a major accident where someone lost their life, or a surprise birthday party where lots of people came and made us feel very special. Secondly, an experience can be powerful if it is a recurring one: our parents fiercely arguing in our presence about a particular topic; or growing up in a home where we were given lots of hugs and messages about how much our parents loved us.

Our collective past experiences will almost always influence the ways in which we approach present situations and how we act with people now. Now analysing ourselves would be a whole lot easier if the more recent the experience, the more weight our subconscious mind gave to it. But it is only our conscious mind that is likely to work in that way, and by definition it will require a conscious act of analysis. For our subconscious, the opposite is usually true: the earlier the experience, the more influential it is likely to be. Centuries ago, one of the most famous men of the early church, Augustine of Hippo, said 'New vessels will for long retain the taste of what is first poured into them.'[1] Although we live in a society of automatic dishwashers we know what he meant! But why is this the case? One very important reason is that children are excellent at observation but poor at interpretation. When a young child is angrily shouted at by a parent, they only feel the force of the anger. The parent may have had a really bad day with dreadful problems at work, or be feeling seriously premenstrual, which was the real source of the anger, and the child was merely a target for adult feelings. But the reasons for the angry outburst would be totally inaccessible for the child. Almost certainly they will have personalised it. And just as nature abhors a vacuum, so children's reason abhors a lack of explanation. The child will try to work out reasons why the parent verbally ripped into them. Their

---

[1] St Augustine, *City of God*, Part 1, Book 1, David Knowles Ed. (Penguin Classics: Harmondsworth 1972). St Augustine is quoting the Roman poet Horace.

conclusion will often be 'I have done something wrong', 'There is something wrong with me', even: 'I'm not a loveable person.' Now the child may have done something wrong, such as leaving a toy in the wrong place. And the parent's reaction may be out of all proportion to the 'crime'. Naturally that may be a correct assessment. What the child will inevitably not come up with is an accurate and balanced analysis of the situation. The child is likely to conclude that there is something wrong them, whereas the correct assessment is simply that the parent is having a bad day. Now if this incident is exceptional, and a one-off, the impact on adult life will probably be minimal; perhaps nothing stronger than a vague feeling of unease when seeing a present-day version of the offending toy. But if the situation was often repeated, the child will, to put it in adult terms, develop coping strategies.

The child's experience begins with observation, which may cause the child pain, discomfort, uncertainty, confusion or some other reaction. If the child recognises the reaction as a fair one this can be a positive step in the child's development. For example, the child breaks something that they have been told not to touch. The child, assuming it is old enough, understands that a parental instruction has been disobeyed. If the punishment is proportionate to the 'crime' and especially if the reason for the punishment is lovingly explained, this may be a positive step in the child learning appropriate obedience. If, however, the punishment is disproportionate to the child's disobedience, even totally unreasonable, then the child seeks to make sense of the punishment and progresses, perhaps immediately, to interpretation. The child's analysis of the gap between their own action and parental response contributes directly into the child's coping strategy. The child is driven to make sense of pain, and come to terms with it. Of course the pain may, for some children, be literal physical pain, but we can also include psychological pain such as confusion, hurt, disempowerment, and a host of other similar feelings.

Different children use different strategies to cope with such pain, although each child may experiment with different strategies until they find one that works for them. So we can define an effective coping strategy *as one that deals with pain better than others.*

Some examples of coping strategies in response to observed situations which are perceived by the child as likely to result in pain are:

- the child who withdraws into himself and becomes silent, trying to keep a low profile or not to be part of the grown-ups' situation (avoidance and dissassociation).
- the little girl whose first response is to rush up to her father, cuddle him and say 'Daddy I love you' (prevention).
- to shout and shout back at parents. This is unlikely to avoid pain but will give the child a sense of empowerment; trying to do something rather than just submitting.

If these or other strategies are relatively effective, they will be branded onto the child's psyche at a very influential stage in its life and will be the first response to problem situations in teenage and adult years. Some adult versions of the above are obvious:

- the adult whose response to problem situations, especially conflict, is to withdraw by either going quiet, or by removing themselves from the situation. This may appear childish, if they shut themselves in the bathroom, or apparently adult if they bury themselves in work.
- the woman who uses her sexuality as a manipulative tool. This may be perceived by others in adult terms as a cynical use of her sexuality but may in fact be a childlike desperation.
- the aggressive adult who likes to 'get their retaliation in first'.

These chilhood experiences will seriously impact how we approach marriage.

The present impact of positive past experiences

These will help us to feel confident, relaxed, competent or not threatened by an awareness of lack of competence in a

particular area; able to cope with pressure, able to give and
receive help, encouragement and love.

The present impact of negative past experiences

These will often tend to make us fearful, defensive, so we retreat
behind barriers, bury feelings, are inappropriately aggressive,
deny that there is a problem, deflect pain by acting or speaking
cruelly to others.

Now of course the above examples should not be pushed too
far! For example, fear can be a very helpful feeling. If we happen
to be standing in front of a runaway bull then fear is a very
appropriate feeling and is likely to prompt us to get out of the
way. By contrast, overconfidence that we can handle the problem without moving out of the way may be heroic but stupid.
The point is more about a sense of fear being unhelpfully intru-
sive, even dominating everyday life and events.

Past experiences can impact on marriage in a variety of ways,
but one in particular is a major source of serious problems. That
is when these experiences become the foundation for our understanding of who and what we are now. Major marital problems
often follow two particular focuses: defining ourselves by our
achievements and defining ourselves by the approval of others.
Although both men and women can be driven by either of
these, and in that sense they are not gender specific; because of a
number of factors in society men tend to be more susceptible to
an over-focus on achievement and women to an over-focus on
approval of others.

An over-focus on achievement

The seeds for this are sown when, as children, we get the
message that we only have significance, or we are only loved,
when we perform well. The ironic thing is that our parents (or
parental figures) may inadvertently cause this seed to grow
from the best of intentions. Wanting to encourage development
in the child, they are praised and emotionally rewarded for

achievement. Without getting into complex educational theory, we know that boys tend to be slower developers than girls and are often lazier. Thus achievement may be explicitly and positively acknowledged and lack of achievement ignored or criticised. This may be in terms of school work, or sports, or constructive hobbies. The subconscious message that can be planted is that we only have value in what we achieve. Picture this example: the ten year old who arrives home at the end of term with a poor report. His mother, knowing that her friend will be boasting about her daughter's glowing achievements, is disappointed. The boy is already feeling bad and his mother's first reaction, driven by her own fears, is to express disappointment. Later, the boy's father, wanting the best for his son, believes that a strong 'you need to pull your socks up' talk is the necessary response to the boy's poor performance. The parents' love may be genuinely unabated, yet the child hears messages not of love and support but criticism for lack of achievement. If the following term he does 'pull his socks up' and receives a better report card, the message is reinforced when the parents greet the improved results with visible signs of approval and love. Although this example is about school work, other examples can easily be surmised for other types of achievements.

In teenage years the person's identity may revolve around academic achievements, sporting abilities, leisure activities, prowess with the opposite sex or even the ability to stand out in a crowd, perhaps being able to make others laugh. By adult years, the person's self-image has become firmly rooted in what they can achieve. For many people the over-focus on achievement transfers directly into career and, specifically, indicators such as job title and salary. This may drive the person to:

- work long hours; not just doing but being seen to try.
- never being satisfied with their present position or status, constantly seeking higher status.
- be uncomfortable about being challenged. Challenge may be interpreted as 'You're failing'. Being unable to handle

criticism or to admit to being wrong: saying, and meaning, 'sorry' may seem almost impossible.

- be overly critical of others. The subconscious aim might be to make it more difficult for others to be in a position to criticise them.

Such people are especially susceptible to what is sometimes known as the Sisyphus complex. Sisyphus was the character in Greek mythology whose task was to push a great heavy rock up to the top of a hill every day, but while he was sleeping at night the stone would be returned to the bottom and he would have to struggle all over again, day after day. People in this mindset put all their energies into getting a particular stone to the top of the hill. Enjoyable things such as fun, quality leisure time, holidays are all postponed until the stone reaches the top. The spouse will be given promises along the lines of 'We'll spend more time together as soon as I have ...' or 'After I have ...'

An over-focus on the approval of others

The seed for this is planted when we grow up with the message that nothing we do is ever good enough. Approval is always qualified in some way. Although there are similarities with an achievement focus, this is significantly different and the learnt message is that we are not entitled to be loved as we are. Again, this may begin with good intentions from the parents. For instance, a girl is told she'd look more pretty if her hair was done differently or if only she was more like 'the nice girl next door.' If these are one-off examples, the message may not be at all damaging but if they are not isolated incidents, then the learnt message will be scored on the girl's personality.

This sense of requiring approval is easily reinforced in puberty and teenage years by the necessity of 'fitting in' with the group, constantly aspiring to project an image: perhaps wearing the 'right' clothes, listening to the 'in' music. Only if these qualifying criteria are met is the person accepted by the peer group. Girls in particular are bombarded with strong messages in teenage years about how, if they want to have a successful relationship with a desirable boy, they must be attractive. And in this they are competing not merely with their peers but music icons and media personalities who have the benefit of professional make-up, unlimited clothes budgets and subtle lighting in posed photographs. Thus the teenager never feels that she has met the absolute standard. At worst this may result in making her sexuality more available as a way of gaining approval, which in time may become counter-productive as the girl becomes labelled by both boys and girls as 'easy'.

In marriage, such a person never feels entirely comfortable because they don't believe they are really loveable or are only loveable if they meet their own exacting standards. Many eating disorders amongst women have their origins in the woman's fear that she is not loveable as she is. Consequently, she has a horror of her husband finding out unpleasant secrets about her and rejecting her. In the case of eating disorders the fear is twofold: 'My husband won't love me until I'm thinner but he won't love me if he suspects I'm bulimic'. One indicator of an over-focus on the approval of others is a tendency to apologise about things which are not her responsibility. Typical compensating behaviour is constantly to seek reassurance that she is loveable. This may be counter-productive as the husband gets increasingly weary of being asked 'Do you love me?' This may lead to pressure on the spouse to demonstrate love and approval in tangible ways. Since the need for approval is not restricted to the spouse, there may well be a tendency to offer to do things for other people, taking on more and more tasks, perhaps even committing their partner to give help to others even when this is not really appropriate. The partner may become exasperated at this, reinforcing the person's sense of being unloveable.

A person with this over approval focus may be like the picnicker constantly looking for the ideal picnic site and never ever finding one. Examples of their typical thought processes are:

- I will be more loveable when I lose some weight.
- I will be more loveable when I have children and proved that I can meet a classic expectation of being a good wife. This can shift to 'When I've had more children.'
- I will be more loveable when I look after the house better.
- I will be more loveable when I can contribute more to the family income.

The Christian in this position may find it very hard to accept that God loves them. They may see God's love as conditional upon their fulfilment of religious duties, such as having regular quiet times, going to church regularly, taking on lots of responsibilities. They will often see themselves as second-class Christians. The great difficulty with the issues that we've been thinking about is that they have become part of our nature for so long, we cannot imagine that things could be any different. To complicate matters further, any self-analysis begins from a point where we are still driven by a longing for achievement or a passion for the approval of others. Even if we desire to shift our focus, the subtle danger is that we simply turn change into one more achievement target or something of which others will approve!

The Process of Change

Misunderstood theology can be a barrier to change. It is important that we do not confuse salvation and holiness. Of course in our unredeemed state we are all far short of God's standards (Romans 3:23). But the New Testament does not teach that we should remain grovelling at the cross. Jesus defines His mission as giving us life in abundance (John 10:10) and elsewhere makes it crystal clear what God's agenda is for our lives: 'Therefore you are to be perfect, as your heavenly Father is perfect.' (Matthew 5:58). If we are to take Paul's image seriously that we have been adopted into God's household (Ephesians 1:5) then the implication is that we have been given the status of princes and princesses. Given our backgrounds, we may know next to nothing about courtly behaviour and the lifestyle of the King, but He wants us to learn. Although the passage is about Jerusalem, a beautiful telling of a similar idea is to be found in Ezekiel 16:1-14.

Another barrier can be the belief that all we need to do is simply to let God live through us. While this contains some important theological truth, it can divert us from the responsibilities that the New Testament places firmly on us. How often do the New Testament writers talk about 'Let go and let God'? Answer: never. Contrast that with the numerous teachings and instructions. We can open Paul almost at random and find him urging us to do things that will contribute to a Kingdom lifestyle. Think how often love is a command and not a promise. Of course, these things don't bring about salvation and the New Testament also makes it clear that God's power is available to help us develop a Kingdom lifestyle. But nowhere are we absolved of the responsibility of taking action.

Once we've got our theology right then we can use it as an important, indeed foundational, starting point. Reflecting on the Biblical truths of what God wants us to be is a mature, adult and spiritually correct counterpoint to the messages that we may have received long ago as children. A helpful thing is to create your own list of Biblical passages that are about what God wants you to be. As a possible starting point here are some example verses: 2 Corinthians 5:17,18; Galatians 4:7; Ephesians 2:10; 1 John 3:1. But reading and reflecting on such verses is not enough in itself. Just to repeat them like some mantra and hope they will sink in is to misunderstand how God uses Scripture. Neither are we called to grit our teeth and try to convince ourselves they ought to be true for us; this is to confuse the Biblical concept of faith with the secular concept of the power of positive thinking. If we have genuine difficulties taking on board what God wants us to be, then we should see such verses as part of God's 'work in progress agenda' for our lives. This should not prompt us to put away the Biblical truth to some point far in the future but recognise that God may well be wanting to work with us on these issues right now. The childhood messages we received have had long years to put down tangled roots in our lives and just pulling up a few leaves is unlikely to kill the whole growth. For that we may need the help of others, which is a Scriptural principle that doesn't always come easily to some of us. The Biblical injunction is: 'Bear one another's burdens and thereby fulfil the law of Christ' (Galatians 6:2). To be able to share our fears and failures with our partner is, in principle, a good thing, not least because they are the best placed to help us through change. But it may be necessary to have the help of pastoral carers or even Christian counsellors, preferably not in place of our partner but in conjunction with them. Two factors should guide us: sadly, the availability, or lack of, wise pastoral care and how serious and deep rooted the issue is. A cut finger may not need medically trained assistance but a serious physical problem will require either the assistance of a first-aider or professional help. Don't forget that even a simple cut may turn septic if not dealt with properly. And it's worth mentioning that if we need medically trained assistance for a physical problem, we recognise that God can work through the skills of such people; we don't usually deny ourselves the benefit of their professional skills and sit around waiting for God to heal us directly. So it is with the type of psychological issues that we've been thinking about. Some issues may be dealt with simply and quickly, even if we need the assistance of a competent bystander: for others we may need more skilled attention.

Ultimately, what we want is for God to heal us. The New Testament should leave us in no doubt that there are times God heals instantly and completely, but responsibility for lifestyle change is ours: 'Go and do not sin again' (John 8:11). However, God seldom chooses to heal instantly. Far more frequent is a gradual healing process, involving our own commitment to change and the love and support of those around us. We can only speculate why God works gradually in these situations, but perhaps one reason is that because these things have become so much a part of who we are, we need time to get used to the change.

How others can help us to change; how we can help others to change

Most of us do not respond positively to aggressive confrontation, even when well meant. How we can best be approached in terms of support to change may give us helpful clues as to a strategy to adopt when aiming to help others. Arguably the best detailed paradigm is how Jesus deals with the woman at the well in John 4. Without compromising God's standards He works through the issues with her gradually and gently, not presenting her with the truth about herself but helping her to discover it for herself. Here are some basic guidelines:

- begin with finding the best opportunity and environment that will enable the other person to open up. This will differ from person to person but almost certainly the worst of all times is when the issue is to the forefront and emotions are running high. The discussion begins best on an empathetic level.
- listen to them. This listening should be done as sympathetically as possible, without judgement, and without trying to counter subjective feelings with objective facts. 'But you shouldn't feel that way' is usually a killer comment, even if intended helpfully. This stage may take a long time as it is about encouraging the person to open up about their hopes and fears, and perhaps to retell some childhood experiences. If done properly, this stage alone may leave both people feeling exhausted.
- address current consequences. If the problem is an over-emphasis on achievement, some reassuring words about loving the person for who they are may be helpful. If the issue is an over-emphasis on approval, then unqualified words of love will be upbuilding, especially if the person has opened up about some of their fears of not being loveable. Emphasis at this point is about being jointly committed to growth and development.

- some form of action plan may be helpful, not with the aim of instant but gradual change. By way of example, some possible action points might be:
  - achievement focus: making gradual changes to lifestyle, such as not bringing work home at weekends.
  - approval focus: the person has to undertake some form of jokey forfeit every time they apologise for something inappropriate.
  - sharing the issue with someone trustworthy from the church perhaps a pastoral team member, and meeting them for prayer.
  - counselling: exploring the possibility of Christian counselling, if the issue is very deeply rooted.

Sometimes, in our growth, just becoming aware of the possibility of change will lead to great advances. In other cases, becoming aware of the matter will not in itself cause change. We may need the help of mature people, lay or professional, or gifted healers who will stand alongside us. God can work through every stage. One of the biggest tragedies that both pastoral carers and Christian counsellors have to deal with is the person who, having become aware of an issue, looks for instant healing, often at some type of healing service. After some immediate euphoria, they become disillusioned when they discover that the problem has not gone away. As we've already emphasised, it is clear that God can heal instantly. But He is not committed to doing so. Our part of the process is to ask for healing, not dictating to God how He should do it.

By way of summary, we will look at a well-known character from the Old Testament. Try to take the opportunity not just to read but to reflect on the growth and development of the individual in question, looking for points of similarity in your own life.

Read Judges 6:11-24

Gideon is a frightened man. That much is obvious from his actions. He is beating out wheat in a wine press. In any conditions it is a hot, dusty job, of necessity done in the open air. While the text doesn't give us details of the day's weather, we can assume a Middle Eastern temperature. Beating the wheat in this way kept the dust cloud a visual secret and thus Gideon safe from the Midianites who would happily steal the wheat, and possibly take Gideon's life into the bargain. The greeting of the angel of the Lord that appears might be prophetic but at this point it seems sarcastic. No doubt the appearance of the angel startled Gideon, but it is not long before he is moaning to the angel about why God has not looked after Israel better. Exactly who addresses Gideon at this point is confusing – it might be the Lord directly or the angel speaking on behalf of the Lord – but either way the responsibility is thrown onto Gideon to rescue Israel. Gideon does not turn round and say something like: 'Okay Lord, here I go.' His self-image very much gets in the way and he lists quite legitimate reasons why he cannot do as commanded. In response, Gideon is given a splendid theological promise (v. 16). Again we can note that this does not prompt Gideon to do what he has been commanded. What comes next appears to be Gideon offering typical Middle Eastern hospitality, although it is offered at a time which gives him the opportunity to delay his response. We might have expected the invitation of hospitality to be given at the beginning rather than at this point, so it is not unreasonable to speculate that Gideon, under the guise of what we might call good manners, plays for time. The description of his meal preparation takes only seconds to read but was, of course, a lengthy process taking perhaps several hours. We can imagine during this time Gideon being deliberately dilatory, hoping that if he takes long enough the angel will have gone away and that he can return to the familiarity of the norm.

Unfortunately for Gideon his visitor is patient. Instead of eating the prepared meal, the angel commands it to be laid on the rock. And Gideon obeys this command without debate. What follows frightens him. Popular theology of the time said that to see an angel would result in death and therefore Gideon expects to die. Any lingering doubts that he may have had about the supernatural status of the visitor vanish, as it were, in a puff of smoke. But in this moment of panic Gideon hears directly from God who assures Gideon of his survival. His response is to build an altar to worship. What we don't see is anything along the lines of Gideon saying: 'Well, after all that, I suppose I'd better get on with rescuing Israel as I was told to do.'

Read Judges 6:25-32

After a powerful worship experience, perhaps with hindsight an immensely enjoyable experience, Gideon may have hoped for things to return to normal. It was not to be. That very night he is given another command; not as exacting as the first but still traumatic enough. The command was in keeping with the Mosaic law but would entail going against family and neighbours. Interpreting the command as loosely as possible, he involves his servants and undertakes the task under the cover of night. His obedience seems to be entwined with the fear of being caught. He accomplishes what has been commanded but this is no great stand of principle. In the morning the secret is soon out; how the people know it was Gideon's doing we are not told but the discovery is quick. Gideon again prepares to die. Given that the pagan altar belonged to his father, we might expect his father to be the most enraged. But stunningly, Gideon is granted protection by his father; a costly about-face as Gideon's father was obviously a man to be listened to. Indeed, it seems as though the action causes Gideon's father to distance himself from Baal worship.

Read Judges 6:33-35

The Spirit of the Lord comes upon Gideon. He sends messengers throughout the country. He is recognised as a national leader. Were it to be said at this point, the angel's greeting in v. 12 would seem legitimate and not the least sarcastic.

Read Judges 6:36-40

The final few verses of this chapter we know as a favourite Sunday school story. But to understand what's going on, let's recap. So far:

- Gideon has had a visit from an angel
- he has witnessed a supernatural event in the form of the offering
- he has been spoken to directly by God
- he has been involved in a powerful worship experience
- he has, reluctantly but successfully, completed a difficult evangelistic mission in his home town
- he has seen what we might think of as the conversion of his own family
- the Spirit of the Lord has come upon him
- he has been recognised as a national leader

Still Gideon's self-imagine cannot cope with what he has been called to do. He asks for a silly sign involving a fleece. We should not read this without a smile on our lips, otherwise we might miss the Hebrew humour based on the absurdity of Gideon's request. We could reasonably expect God to tell Gideon not to be so silly and get on with his mission. But God doesn't. Despite all that has gone before, God puts His timescale on hold and meets Gideon's request. Still Gideon is not satisfied! He pleads for the reverse of what has taken place. Once again God complies. Fully to understand this, personalise it: suppose you were commanded to do something but you are offered a sign. You can choose:

a visit from an angel; a powerful supernatural experience; a radically new worship experience; a successful mission in your home town involving the conversion of your family; the Spirit of the Lord coming upon you; being recognised as a national Christian leader; or a fleece that stays dry when everything else is wet or is wet when everything else is dry?

Which would you choose? And which would be at the bottom of your list?

Yet it is the silly incident with the fleece that changes Gideon. Why it is the breakthrough issue we don't know; perhaps something to do with a fleece from an influential childhood moment? Before that Gideon was presented with theological truth, divine promises, ministry success and several other things. None of them really changed his self-image. It was through an apparently trivial incident that Gideon was changed. No more do we hear of excuses from him. He goes on to be a valiant warrior who rescues Israel. His background, his emotional baggage had been a serious obstacle. The healing occurred in a remarkable way. Just as we can expect God to work through the 'important' things, so we should expect that He will also heal via the trivial.

Questions

1. To which do you think you are more susceptible: an over-focus on achievement or an over-focus on the approval of others? To which do you think your partner is more susceptible?

2. Thinking about your self-image: what are your particular fears?

3. (a) Are there any particular experiences from the past that you think might especially be impacting on the present in unhelpful ways:
   (i) From childhood
   (ii) From teenage years
   (iii) From a previous relationship

(b) What can you do to diminish their impact? How can you best obtain the help of your partner?

4. Reflect on Matthew 5:48 and John 10:10. How do you think God wants you to see yourself?

What am I? What are You?

How our personalities affect our marriage

Having thought in some detail about how our past experiences impact on the present, we can now give some related thought to how our personalities affect the day-to-day aspects of marriage. Identifying the importance of past experiences should not only lead to greater understanding of one another but may also indicate some areas for personal development and possibly healing. The consideration of personality differences is more about gaining a sympathetic understanding of one another. The challenge is not so much about individual change but how, as a couple, we can harmonise our differences for the good of the relationship.

Most people are fascinated by personality profiling. We enjoy the opportunity to discover more about who and what we are, even if we are sceptical about the results. Perhaps the origins again go back to earliest childhood, when we defined ourselves in relation to others: the child of our parents; someone's brother or sister; a member of Miss Smith's class at school. But perhaps our first exposure to anything resembling personality profiling were the surveys that fill teenage magazines. They have attention grabbing titles such as 'Are you attractive to the opposite sex?' A vital question to most teenagers! There might follow a series of, say, ten questions with a, b or c responses. The results would then be simple groupings. For example: 'If you've got seven or more a's then you'll need to keep a diary of all your many dates; if you've got seven or more b's then you probably need to get out more and meet a wider variety of people; if you've got seven or more c's …' Well, if we got seven or more c's we'd probably stop reading at that point in despair. No matter how pleasing our results in such surveys, we probably didn't take them too seriously, recognising that they were not very scientific. Nevertheless, we probably were interested enough to do them anyway, justifying it as 'just a bit of fun.'

Personality profiling is used in a wide variety of contexts, including the business world and various forms of counselling. There are a range of tests: some are fairly basic, whereas others are complex and require special training. To complicate matters for the untrained person, different profiling techniques are based on different psychological models, so comparing results from different tests is not only unwise, it is also usually fairly pointless. At worst, the tests are misused to pigeon-hole people. At best, they provide insights in the form of raw data that suggest typical patterns but, more importantly, offer detailed agenda for discussion. The most important outcome from a correctly administered process is not the test results themselves but the debriefing based on the test results. One implication of this is that while self-administered tests from self-help books can often provide useful insights, the results should not be relied upon to any great extent. The real value is to be gained from systematic reflection on, and discussion about, what the results indicate.

In a marriage context, personality profiling can obviously provide very useful opportunities for a better understanding of ourselves and our partner. The catch is that most couples don't have the opportunity to do such tests together, and even if one of them has done such a test, say at work, subsequent discussion will be lopsided. For the reasons discussed above, it is not feasible to reproduce a profiling test here. As a substitute, below are a series of questions that can be done together. It's best to copy the chart onto a separate sheet of paper and then compare your results.

Remember

- What is important is the subsequent discussion, not the actual marks. In any case the marks are based on gut reaction rather than anything very objective.
- There are no right and wrong, better or worse, with regard to preferences.
- The categories below are simplified.
- Personality preferences are not necessarily indicators of behaviour.
- Accurate personality profiling takes a long time. It is not an end in itself but an agenda for discussion and understanding.

Instructions

Below are four areas. There are two or three questions related to each area. Mark on the line where you guess you and your partner's natural preferences are in response to each question or statement. When marking your partner's reaction, what you're guessing is their answer to the question, not their response to your answer. If you find you totally and unreservedly agree with one of the options then you should mark at the extreme end of the particular line. Example:

(a) _____ (b)

Self   Partner

But in most cases you will probably find you want to qualify your response. That's fine; simply mark on the line at what seems to be an appropriate point. Example:

(a) _____●_____●_____ (b)

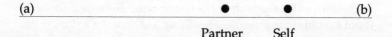

                        Partner   Self

Area 1: Living space: is your tendency towards introversion or extroversion?

1. You've had a tough and highly pressurised day. It seems like anything that could go wrong has gone wrong. But you have the evening to yourself; your partner is away for the night. You have no particular commitments and you can spend the evening as you wish. What's your response to your tough day? Do you:
    a) Park the car round the corner so you don't appear to be in; unplug the phone; make sure no lights are showing at the front of the house, in other words doing everything you can to avoid any interaction with anyone else.
    b) Feel that because you've had a tough day, you need to unwind with other people and make a point of getting together with others.

(a) _____ (b)

2. It's that moment after Sunday morning church when the last prayer has been prayed, the last hymn sung and people are about to start milling about. What's your reaction? Do you:
    a) Dread this moment because you never quite know how to chat with people and can't think of anything to say? Even if you stay around out of a sense of Christian duty, do you really long to escape as soon as possible.
    b) Regard this is the real highlight of the morning, when you have a chance to zoom around and catch up with a variety of people; you wish the after-service time could go on longer.

(a) _____ (b)

Area 2: vision? will it work?

1. How do you respond to facts and firm data? Do you:
    a) Find facts and data reassuring. You are at your happiest in terms of decision-making when a decision can be reduced to a fact or formula. You see the absolute truth in terms of facts.
    b) Distrust raw facts and data. Believe that to discover real truth you have to look behind facts, read between the lines. Believe that raw facts and data can often be misleading.

(a) _____ (b)

2. Imagine you have a project at home: perhaps a major redecoration project, or remodelling the garden. Do you:
    a) Focus primarily on practical questions such as how much will it cost, how long will it take, how worthwhile will it be, and then plan the project accordingly.
    b) Focus on the potential, and give full scope to the creative possibilities.

(a) _____ (b)

Area 3: judgement or mercy?

1. Imagine that you are working for a company and you are in charge of a small team of four people. The five of you get on well together and function as an effective team. One morning you are called into your line manager's office. They inform you that the company is going through a tough time financially and one of your team must be made redundant. The decision as to who shall be made redundant is left up to you. What are your first thoughts? Do you:

a) Think about who is least likely to damage the effectiveness of the team; who will be missed the least.
b) Think about the needs and circumstances of the individuals concerned, focusing on such questions as who will best survive being made redundant; who most needs the job.

(a)   (b)

2. Imagine that you are responsible for a group of about twenty children of junior school age. (Say, for example, at a church event.) You want the children to have a good time. At the beginning of the day, you lay down appropriate rules and regulations, and make clear you will punish anyone who breaks the rules. After a while, one of the children obviously and publicly breaks one of the rules. Immediately one of the teenager helpers who is working with you explains that there are mitigating circumstances why the child did what they did. Do you:
a) Take on board that the child couldn't help breaking the rule, but decide for the sake of justice being done and being seen to be done, that the punishment must go ahead anyway. You resolve to be as loving as possible to the child in question but implement the punishment.
b) On the grounds that the child could not help what they did, let the child off being punished.

(a)   (b)

Area 4: structured or unstructured?

1. You are on holiday and have the opportunity of visiting somewhere you'll never have the chance to see again. When you arrive at the entrance a free guide book is available, which gives a prescribed route, suggesting the best order in

which to view things, how long to spend at each point, and so on. To make the best use of the opportunity do you:

a) Follow the guidebook rigidly and with enthusiasm.

b) Make a point of not even taking a copy of the guidebook and wander as the whim takes you.

(a)   (b)

2. You are a member of a project committee. You are happy to be part of it; the team is working well together and the project is progressing smoothly. The chairperson produces a careful agenda and keeps the discussion strictly to the agenda. At the next meeting you discover the chairperson is ill and the vice-chairperson takes over the running of the meeting. They beginning by saying: 'Things have been going well but I believe we can make even faster progress. We all know each other well and what the issues are. At this meeting we'll ignore the published agenda and just speak about the issues as we see them.' Is your reaction:

a) Immediate frustration, convinced that the meeting will be a total waste of time.

b) An immediate sense of liberation, optimistic that the meeting will be more effective and more enjoyable.

(a)   (b)

3. It's the start of the weekend. You and your partner have the shared expectation that the weekend is likely to involve a combination of some routine tasks and some relaxation. Do you:

a) Make a list, either together or individually, of things that you want to achieve over the weekend, including the leisure elements.

b) Not make a list under any circumstances and politely but firmly tell your partner what to do with such a list if they try and commit you to one.

(a)   (b)

Before discussing your answers ...

As we've already emphasised, the above guesstimates will not give you a definitive profile result. But if you and your partner have answered as honestly as possible, then you've certainly got a lot of food for thought. Comparing your answers can spontaneously generate topics for discussion and these will be fruitful to explore. But before doing that it will be helpful to think about some general issues related to each area.

Area 1 issues

As their name implies, personality profiles are designed to test personality preferences, not behaviour. A person can have a strong preference in one area but behave – either by choice or circumstance – quite differently. An example of this can often be observed in counselling some newly married couples. Typically one person (we'll say the man) is by nature fairly introverted. But, possibly quite subconsciously, he puts himself in group social situations. This is how he meets his future wife and they find themselves, as many going-out couples do, spending quite a lot of time with other people. Although this is not his natural territory, he's content to be there for a variety of obvious reasons. He may well role-play extroversion as a coping mechanism. Others mistake his role-playing for his natural personality, little realising that the emotional cost for him is actually quite high. Once married, he changes. At first his wife assumes that it's just circumstances being different but gradually she accuses him of change; being less outgoing, perhaps being anti-social, much quieter. She may not like this change, especially if she is an extrovert. This may lead to criticism of her husband or even self criticism, wondering if he is disappointed that he's married her. Ironically the opposite may be the case. He may feel very comfortable with her and now feels free to be the person he really is. The accusation 'You've changed' is both true and false. His behaviour has changed but what has really changed is the wife's perception of who her husband really is. What they should do about it is an important question that we need not deal with in detail here. Once they have become aware of the real issue, then they can discuss the implications together. Both may need to adjust their behaviour for the sake of each other. Before leaving this example, it's worth mentioning that introverts will often be attracted to extroverts, because they bring to the partnership a social skill that the introvert lacks. An introvert's worst nightmare is usually a cocktail party situation; an extrovert partner can get them through it together.

Another example is where a person with a personality tending towards introversion is required to work in an extrovert context. Common examples are schoolteachers and people whose work involves a great deal of people interaction. When they come home from work their reaction, at least until they have wound down a bit, is to need even greater introversion levels than their actual introversion would suggest. This we call the ping-back factor. If you stretch elastic from a fixed point, when released it may at first ping-back beyond its fixed point. The ping-back factor can be observed in extroverts whose day requires them to have little people interaction: perhaps being alone in an office, or sitting in front of a computer for most of the day. When they come home, they will be desperate for interaction.

Understanding one's own personality can result in better understanding of other people. The person the extrovert thought of as anti-social or stand-offish may turn out to be a very nice person, but introverted. The person the introvert thought of as unbearable and needing to be the centre of attention may also be a very nice person who is an extrovert.

Area 2 issues

Vision is thought of as a good thing, and usually it is. Vision is needed to spot potential and better ways of doing things. However, visionaries are not always great at spotting problems; at worst they are not interested in considering obstacles. In church contexts people with a strong personality bias towards vision can accuse people who ask 'will it work?' questions of having a lack of faith. In fact the difference is often not a spiritual one but about personality. No-one could seriously accuse Jesus of not advocating faith but He also taught the importance of asking 'will it work?' questions (Luke 14:25–32).

People whose personality leads them naturally to ask 'will it work?' can make assumptions about visionaries! They will assume that they have taken into account 'will it work?' factors, when in fact the questions may not have even occurred to them. So an encounter may go something like this:

Person 1 says: 'I'm going to decorate the spare room this weekend.' [Based on thought: 'I can imagine that the spare room would look great redecorated. I've got several hours spare. It shouldn't take that long to paper the walls. Oh, the ceiling and doors may need painting but that's quick …']

Person 2 thinks: ['That's a huge job. It'll take hours just to clear all the stuff out. The old wallpaper in there will be really hard to get off. And when the old paper is stripped off, it will probably be like the other bedroom where there were a lot of repairs to be done before we could paper. Oh, and it will take a long time to get to the DIY shop because of Saturday traffic. Still, I suppose they've thought all this through.'] Says: 'Well, if you're sure …'

Late on Sunday evening, when the room is a long way from completion:

Person 2 says: 'I suppose we'll have to live with this chaos until next weekend, and you'll have to spend next weekend finishing it off, even though my parents were due to visit. I knew it would take you longer than you said.'

Person 1 says: 'Why didn't you say? I thought it would only take a few hours. I thought it would look so nice for when your parents come.'

As with many differences, if a couple have different personality tendencies in this area, either it can become a battleground or the strengths can be united to make an effective combination, providing the challenging is done sensitively. The visionary can learn to hear, and take into account, 'will it work?' questions; the person with a 'will it work?' tendency can learn to see that problems do not always have to be insurmountable obstacles and that there is a time for taking calculated risks.

Area 3 issues

Most people instinctively want to mark their answer some-where in the middle of the line. While that may be possible for the question on redundancy, an answer in the middle with regard to the looking after children raises the valid question of what would such an answer look like in practice? Any attempt to live out an answer in the middle would almost certainly be some form of compromised botch. By their very nature, justice and mercy are mutually exclusive. We can have either but not both at the same time. A well-known example is in the book by Victor Hugo (or more familiarly, the musical) *Les Misérables*. Much of the story is about the impossibility of harmonising justice and mercy. If we read through the Old Testament we observe a continual tension between these two things. We find many of the Psalms unpalatable precisely because the Psalmist cries for justice, and he recognises that if he is to receive justice inevitably his enemy must receive punishment. In marriage it is crucial to keep this problem in mind when it comes to raising children. If one parent has a tendency to mercy and the other justice, the child will receive mixed messages and at worst will be able to play one parent off against the other. Each parent will feel let down or betrayed by the other. A discipline strategy, worked out in advance of actual problems, is crucial when parents are at opposite ends of this line.

In this whole area there is huge potential for getting it wrong. Mistakes and clashes will occur. Being aware of each others' personalities will help enormously. What will also help is to keep the following in mind: what we've said above about justice and mercy being mutually exclusive is almost, but not quite, true. Once, and only once, they met perfectly and without compromise: at Golgotha. The actual cost of them meeting perfectly is really beyond our comprehension, and our best response is worship.

Area 4 issues

It's possible to have hours and hours of philosophical debate about the advantages and disadvantages of structured versus unstructured lifestyles. In marriage, if both partners are much the same then the problems related to personality differences will not occur. The problems arise when one partner is structured and the other is unstructured. Understanding is crucial, not just of the person's personality preference but also the cost to them in adjusting their behaviour. It's in this area partners have immense scope to infuriate one another. For example, structured people will generally be punctual; unstructured people are frequently unpunctual. The former will often ask in exasperated tone: 'Why can't you be on time for once?' The question assumes that being on time is easy to arrange, as it's easy for the questioner. For the unstructured person, the emotional effort is much greater. This is not to say that they shouldn't make it; the point is the structured person needs to understand the cost of the effort.

Of course there is a place for deep understanding and behaviour adjustment in this whole area, but generally sensitive humour will go a long way to dispel any real problems before they start. For example, we can easily see the difference between the structured and the unstructured person in their attitude to lists. The structured person will see lists as liberating; the unstructured person will see them as a strait-jacket. What are the signs of a true list maker? Firstly, they cannot believe that lists are a problem! They will often say things like: 'But you have to make lists.' What they really mean is that they have to. The true list maker is someone who makes lists while on holiday and someone who, if they do something not on their list, will write the item on the list and immediately cross it off! Such actions can be infuriating but can also, when viewed with understanding, be endearing features. Unstructured partners can benefit greatly from structured partners, if they permit them to have appropriate control over processes. The list maker will know to whom they should send Christmas cards, when birthdays are, and suchlike. Many self-help books emphasise the great benefits of effective habits and lists. But the structured partner can benefit from the life approach of an unstructured partner. For there are times when lists are restrictive. They can put a break on spontaneity. The list maker may not get around to 'fun' because it's not the sort of thing that gets put on a list. Following a pre-planned route may mean that you fail to come across the charming little café.

Questions

1. What are the implication of your results for your relationship?

2. Are there things that your partner does which infuriate you? Do they seem unable to change although to you such change seems a simple thing to ask? Might the reason be personality differences?

3. Do your results suggest that there are particular issues that you ought to explore in order to understand each other better?

The Problem of Forgiveness?

Forgiveness is a subject about which we hear quite a bit these days in many areas of life. It is also a familiar subject in Christian teaching. We recognise its importance and we know both in theory and from experience that forgiveness ought to be part of our relationships. But if we're frank, we may be left with some unanswered questions and, more seriously, a sense that we've tried to forgive but that it just hasn't worked. Some well-known Biblical passages reinforce our theoretical commitment to forgiveness but their uncompromising nature may give rise to guilt and a feeling of personal failure if we've tried forgiving. Lack of forgiveness of people from our past and in present relationships can be a major block to us being the person God wants us to be, and having the marriage that He wants us to have. However, our aim is not to raise the guilt levels in order to 'have another go' at forgiving; rather, it is to think about obstacles to our forgiving and to gain fresh insights into ways forward.

What is forgiveness, and why forgive?

The first obstacle to our forgiving is that we may not really have understood what the Bible means by forgiveness, and how it relates to other issues such as repentance and restoration. To get a handle on this, let's consider two different stories:

Derek and Mark

Derek has offered to help his friend Mark move some stuff into his new flat. While they are both carrying heavy boxes up the stairs, Mark gets careless and a box falls on Derek's foot. It hurts badly and Derek wonders if his foot is broken. Mark immediately apologises, confesses to having been careless and promises to be more careful. He asks for Derek's forgiveness, and Derek gives it. Derek continues helping Mark but with a limp!

The next morning Derek's foot is very sore when he wakes up. It's obviously not broken but it is badly bruised. He realises that he will not be able to play in the football match that he's been looking forward to.

Marion and Clare

Marion has been invited to join a project group in her church. The group has been formed to consider and start up a new women's outreach group. Marion often has good ideas but is a quiet, shy person who finds it difficult to say very much in groups. She has wanted to be more involved in church for many months but no one in leadership had seemed to notice her. So she really wants to take the opportunity of 'making her mark' as part of this group. Marion's friend Clare is also part of the group. Unlike Marion, Clare is outgoing and confident, always invited to take part in events. As both live a few miles away from the church, Clare offers to pick Marion up and take her to her to the first meeting.

The meeting is due to begin at 8.00. By 7.00 Marion is ready and waiting, even though Clare said she'd arrive about 7.30. At 7.50 Marion is panicking that they are going to be late. By 8.10 she overcomes her shyness and telephones Clare, who had forgotten about the meeting, despite Marion having reminded her earlier that day. Clare eventually picks Marion up and they arrive at the meeting nearly an hour late. Clare, who knows everyone there very well, breezes in and quickly joins in. She jokes that she was late because she had to pick up Marion. Marion is embarrassed and sits very quietly. The discussion has identified various roles for which people need to take responsibility. Marion would love to take on responsibility but she is too shy to volunteer. Most are allocated quickly to people already doing other things in the church. Finally, one role is left to be filled, a role Marion knows she could do very well. The chairwoman says: 'Ideally this is something that it would be good for a new person to do. But' – and here she looks pointedly at Marion – 'they must be reliable; punctuality is crucial. Clare,

I wonder if you'd like to take this on?' Clare says something about being quite busy but that she's happy to give it a go. Marion fights back tears.

In the journey back home Clare apologises to Marion for being late. She asks Marion to forgive her. Marion, not wanting to damage her relationship with Clare expresses her forgiveness. In bed that night she still feels let down by Clare and so wonders if she really has forgiven her.

The next Sunday the chairwoman tells the church about the new project and introduces the team, telling the church who is doing what. She forgets to mention Marion. Marion feels upset and annoyed with Clare. She feels guilty about still feeling resentful towards Clare.

Some points:

- Mark admits his mistake and promises to be more careful. He asks for forgiveness which Derek gives. So the process is: confession; repentance; asking for forgiveness; giving of forgiveness; restoration of relationship. Does this stop Derek's foot hurting? Of course not! The consequences of the action remain; in this case, physical pain.
- Would we expect Derek to feel resentment or something similar towards Mark for having to miss his football match as a result of his friend's carelessness? Probably. This doesn't mean he hasn't forgiven him.
- In what ways is Marion's situation like Derek's? Her pain is a result of a friend's carelessness. In some ways, Clare's actions are worse than Mark's because Clare could have done more to put the problem right. Just as we wouldn't expect Derek's forgiving of Mark instantly to heal his bruised foot, neither should we expect Marion's forgiveness to deal with her emotional pain.
- Will Mark and Clare remember to ask their friends how they are after the event? Will Clare consider how Marion felt during the chairwoman's report back to the church? Are there additional things for which ideally they should ask their friends' forgiveness?

The forgiveness process

We can identify some important principles that make up the forgiveness process:

- Ideally, forgiveness is a response to a request for forgiveness; that is, an acknowledgement that something has happened to damage the relationship and a desire to avoid either a temporary or permanent rift.
- Forgiveness may well restore the relationship but this does not cause pain and consequences to vanish. Forgiveness does not automatically bring about instant healing.
- Forgiveness may need to be repeated for similar offences, even though we might hope the offender will have 'learnt their lesson.'
- There are times when, even if forgiveness is asked for, the offended person may not be in a position to give it.

Let's think about what is the ideal process when something has gone wrong in a relationship. By ideal we mean a process that includes all the theological elements.

Phase 1

(a) A recognition by the offender that they have done something which causes some form of damage, for example physical or emotional hurt, to another person.

(b) An attempt at understanding the significance and level of the damage to the person, recognising that the level of hurt may bear no relationship whatsoever to our motives or intentions.

(c) A determination to contain the damage and to try to ensure that the overall relationship is not harmed.

(d) Repenting of the thing that caused the initial damage.

Phase 2

Communicating the above to the injured person in a way that is helpful and meaningful; in a way they can best understand rather than the way that makes us feel most comfortable; being sensitive to time, place and other circumstances.

Phase 3

Asking for forgiveness: again, in a way that is helpful and meaningful to the other person.

Phase 4

Restoration: attempting to put right the specific damage originally caused and to repair the relationship fully, even if consequences from the original damage remain. We can think of the purpose of forgiveness as restoration of the relationship. The above assumes that there is a genuine commitment and motive. This is not simply a formula to be voiced.

It is important to recognise that if we have done something that hurts another person, then it is likely that emotions will be running high. That is why it is so important to give due regard to the emotional state of the person we have offended. The temptation is to try and put things right in a time and manner with which we are comfortable, whereas the loving thing is to do it in a way that is helpful to the other person. By definition, this may cause us discomfort. For example, if we are the type of person who likes to 'strike while the iron is hot' then we may want to act immediately. But the person may not be in the best place to hear us. We may need to learn to wait for a bit. Or perhaps we are the opposite, reflecting for a long time before taking action. Then we may need to communicate at an earlier point than one with which we are naturally comfortable.

Some helpful and unhelpful phrases

The exact words in the examples below are not the crucial point:
that is the meanings and tone that these examples represent.

Helpful Phrases	Unhelpful Phrases
I didn't mean to hurt you but I can see I've upset you.	I don't know why you're so upset. I didn't mean to hurt you.
Is now a good time to talk about this or would you prefer some space for a while?	Let's get this sorted out right away.
I genuinely don't understand why what I've done has hurt you. But I would like to understand. Please help me to do that.	You're getting this way out of proportion. Get a grip on yourself.
Let's talk about it so we can move on.	Let's forget about it and move on.
I'm sorry for ...	I'm sorry but ...
I'm sorry about what happened. Is there anything I can do?	I'm sorry about what happened but I can't undo it.
I'm sorry I hurt you. Although I hope you know this anyway, I want to make sure that you know that I didn't mean it. Although this is part of my character, it's part of me I'd like to change.	I'm sorry that I hurt you but you know I didn't mean it. It's just my character.

Forgiveness and feelings

One all too common problem in forgiving someone is that we
assume that if we genuinely forgive them then our emotions
will be in harmony with the act, and we will no longer experience feelings such as anger, resentment and bitterness towards
them. If we still feel some or all of these things, we conclude that

we didn't really forgive the person, and we enter the downward loop of forgiving again, still feeling negative things, forgiving again, and so on, like an aircraft, out of control, spiralling towards the ground. The way to break out of this dive to destruction is to recognise that initially we need to separate out the act of forgiveness from our feelings. *The feelings will usually be connected to the consequences of the act against us, rather than our act of forgiving.* The more hurtful or painful the act against us was, the more powerful the associated feelings and emotions will be. Just as in our previous example, forgiveness did not cause the pain to vanish, neither would annoyance or anger towards Mark, who dropped the box for being so careless. This is not to say that we should be resigned to always harbouring negative and unhelpful feelings. Forgiveness will open the door to them being dealt with as well, but not necessarily immediately. They may need time, sometimes a great deal of time if the hurt is great, to catch up with forgiveness having taken place. This is one of those examples where an understanding of the idea communicated by the original Greek of the New Testament will be of great help.

For most of us, our earliest memory of Scripture would be learning the Lord's prayer. For many of us that meant the old Prayer Book version that begins:

'Our Father who art in heaven, Hallowe'd be thy name.'
It later includes:

'Forgive us our trespasses as we forgive those who trespass against us.' We probably learnt to recite the words long before we understood them and our earliest understanding is unlikely to have given due consideration to the weight of the meaning of the old English word trespass! If we thought about it at all, we probably associated it with the idea of physical trespass, as in the familiar sign; 'trespassers will be prosecuted'. Therefore we had a vague sense of asking God to forgive us when we strayed into inappropriate areas; seeing them as misdemeanours rather than anything major. The actual Greek of Matthew 6:12 conveys a much stronger idea (although we ought to recognise that the actual Greek is difficult because of a rare construction – hence the footnote variations and different translations).[1] Jesus' words in Matthew 6:12 can literally be understood as: 'Forgive us our debts, as we forgive those who are in debt to us.' The Jews were fond of thinking of sin as a debt and so the obvious implication is that debt includes the idea of sin; or to put it another way, an offence. This clause of the prayer therefore recognises that just as we incur debts with God, so people who have wronged us are in debt to us. What may make us uncomfortable here is that the prayer, from Jesus' very lips, seems to suggest that God forgiving us is conditional on our forgiving others. We cannot get away from this plain implication of Jesus' words, but this should not prompt us to throw away Paul's teaching on justification by faith and salvation being a free gift from God. What Jesus is talking about here is not primarily how we enter into a relationship with God but the ongoing quality of that relationship. Unforgiveness towards others will not only damage our relationship with them but also our relationship with God.

When we see forgiveness in terms of forgiving a debt, it probably reminds us of the parable of the unforgiving servant in Matthew 18:23–35, where again we see Jesus emphasising the importance of forgiveness in no uncertain terms. We must not forget that Jesus is teaching here in parables. We cannot unthinkingly equate the king of the parable with God. We are intended to note a particular point of similarity, not an exact likeness. In the parable the king forgives the servant a vast amount of money. The amount is so huge we might wonder in passing what on earth the servant did with what amounts to tens of millions of pounds. But it is an important part of the

---

[1] For anyone wondering why the Greek is complex, a basic summary is that it is not clear when examining all manuscript traditions if the clause should be understood as: 'because we have forgiven others' [an action in the past]; 'because we are forgiving others' [an ongoing action in the present] or 'so that we can forgive others' [an future action to follow on from our forgiveness]. There are other complexities but to go into them here would be to get away from how we should understand the clause in practical terms.

parable that we do not know. The king's forgiveness is not conditional on how the servant used the money but upon the servant's plea for forgiveness and the king's compassion. The point is: the king forgives the debt. But, as we know, the servant fails to forgive a much smaller debt, a day's wage of a labourer. The first servant's relationship with the king is conditional on the servant mirroring the king's compassion in the form of forgiving the debt owed to him. The consequence of not doing so is personal pain. Some modern translations sanitise the end. In fact the king hands the unforgiving servant over to the torturers, which is one reason we shouldn't push the parallel between the king and God too far. Nevertheless, modern medicine recognises that harbouring unforgiveness can result in a variety of unpleasant medical conditions, both psychological and physical.

Recognising that these two passages of Scripture require us to practise forgiveness as if we are releasing someone from a debt, raises the question of exactly how we should go about it. What follows is simply one way of forgiving that has helped a number of people in counselling situations; it is not intended to be a definitive method and if it isn't helpful, abandon it and seek some other method.

Step 1

Acknowledge to yourself the extent of your hurt. This may be relatively easy for some people whereas others will deny, or partly deny, the hurt.

Step 2

Identify the thing or things that have been taken from you: that is, the debt. Be as specific as possible. For example, if your partner is constantly unpunctual, you may feel robbed of time, peace and being seen by others in a good light. Obviously serious issues, such as being a victim of child abuse, may have many facets such as being robbed of childhood innocence and joy, innocent cuddles from adults as well as the more obvious issues such as virginity and being able to sleep peacefully at night.

Step 3

(a) Make a conscious decision to release the offender from the debt they owe you, recognising that it is often impossible for them to give you back what they have taken from you. Even if they repent and desire restoration, the things of which you feel robbed may be gone forever. In the above examples the unpunctual partner cannot repay time you've already lost; childhood innocence cannot be returned.

(b) One way of doing this that some people find helpful is to write down what has been lost. It can be done in the form of an invoice made out in the offender's name. This can, as a conscious act of will, be torn up, or perhaps have 'Released' written across it.

Step 4

Be clear about what you have and haven't done.

You have:

- Done what is commanded in Scripture, so you can be confident that what you've done is in line with God's will. Thus other parts of the process are now, so to speak, God's problem, not yours.
- Undertaken an act of will that doesn't necessarily have any immediate effect on your emotions, although of course it might do so.

You haven't:

- Condoned the original offence or implied that it doesn't really matter.
- Tried to pretend that the offender is a nice person when they may have done something truly evil.

- Dealt with all the related issues; just forgiveness. For example, you may still need to experience some form of healing and there may be outstanding restitution.

Of course we must apply common sense! It is hardly necessary to go through these steps for minor offences. If somebody accidentally steps on your toe and apologises, then you can probably forgive them quickly and easily. The above steps are for those offences, apparently big or apparently small, that for whatever reason affect us powerfully and are difficult to forgive.

How do repentance and restoration fit in with forgiveness?

If the person who has caused the offence asks for our forgiveness and thus demonstrates repentance coupled with the aim of trying to put right what has been damaged, then the issues are clear enough. But what about the person who doesn't, or won't, acknowledge that they have done something wrong? Or perhaps they can't? They may be a figure from our distant past, maybe no longer alive. It's in such situations that our feelings and emotions may have the most difficulty in being in harmony with the act of forgiving. In these instances, it is often helpful to be aware that forgiveness is the part of the process for which we can take responsibility. We do not have to let the hurt disempower us in this important spiritual area. We can still release the person from the debt they unknowingly owe us, but the full benefit of forgiveness, that is restoration of the relationship, may not be available in any meaningful form – although feeling at peace with the memory of the person may still be of some benefit. One thing such forgiveness will do is enable us to pray for that person with greater compassion. It may be that after going through the conscious act of forgiving an absent person for an old or unacknowledged hurt, we remain aware of feelings of resentment and bitterness. One thing that may help is to reflect on what damage may have been caused to them that we've never noticed or considered, as our feelings were getting in the way of viewing their life with godly compassion. What we heard and felt at the time as serious hurt, may in fact have been their own pain communicating to us. Learning to see others from God's perspective is of great value. It would be easier if we could do it before forgiving so that forgiveness would seem so much easier. But, in fact, it is when we forgive that we can see things more clearly. Then we see the Lord's prayer works both ways: as we become more aware of God's love for us, and how much He has forgiven us, we can begin to mirror that love towards those that have offended us.

Before leaving this area we must anticipate a question. If we have experienced the love and forgiveness of God for ourselves, shouldn't we naturally, or rather supernaturally, want to forgive others? This is a yes and a no! No doubt when we are truly Christlike, forgiveness will flow from us as it did from Jesus towards the soldiers who were banging nails through the sensitive nerves of his hands and feet (Luke 23:34). But most of us are nowhere near that point yet. Just as we have much to learn in other areas of love and compassion, so it is with forgiveness. Unlike Jesus, we may find it difficult to communicate love, compassion and forgiveness when someone is causing us great pain. We need time to come to terms with our hurt.

Forgiveness in marriage

It is generally recognised that the more we love someone, the more they are capable of hurting us. The displeasure of our partner affects us far more than the displeasure of a stranger that we'll never see again. Closely twinned with this is the obvious reality that because our partner is the person we are closest to in terms of day-to-day living, then marriage, more than any other relationship, is likely to give rise to more issues requiring forgiveness. The danger is that we can neglect to address the issues properly because we take each other for granted; the 'But why are you upset? You know I didn't mean to hurt you' approach. The problem is often caused by measuring the issue in the wrong way. We're apt to measure the issue by the significance of the offence, whereas what really needs to be evaluated is the amount of hurt caused. This may not be directly proportionate to the actual offence but may be linked to a host of other things, such as the offence opening up issues from the past. It is vital that forgiveness is not neglected in marriage. We can probably think of older couples whose marriage appears more like an ongoing truce than a loving relationship, where any disagreement escalates quickly into a serious row, bringing up past offences from previous years. Such marriages have been slowly poisoned by unforgiveness.

We've already thought about the Lord's Prayer and how we've probably known it since early childhood. Our very familiarity can inoculate us against seeing the bigger picture of Matthew 6:7-14; we need to read it with adult insight. Jesus introduces the prayer by telling us not to pray like the Gentiles; in this case, a people who do not know God. He presents these people as praying like an advocate in court. The idea here is that if the person can put a strong enough case before the judge, then the hope is that the judge will either let them off or give them what they want. Hence the need for 'many words', and the person will plead every mitigating fact and circumstance. By contrast, the Christian's prayer is to be based on the knowledge of God's character and omnipotence. Ultimately, God's forgiveness is a product not of the strength of our pleading but on His character and the relationship we have with Him. In turn, we are to mirror that in our relationship with others; just as the forgiven servant should have mirrored the king's forgiveness to his fellow servant. We can extend this principle to marriage without implying an exact parallel. When one partner does something wrong, incurs a debt with their partner, how easy it is to plead our case: 'I didn't mean it'; 'I wasn't concentrating'; 'It's because it's that time of the month'; 'You know I'm quick-tempered'; 'But I thought you said ...' and so on. We can always find justifications for minimising our guilt and thus trying to reduce the debt. It's as though the sub-text is: 'Okay, I admit to a certain amount of guilt but I want you to take the following data into account and thus reduce my culpability.' If, however, we apply the Lord's prayer principle here, then we must put such pleading to one side. Instead of trying to minimise our guilt, the emphasis should be on asking for forgiveness, owning up to the full effect of our actions and taking responsibility for them. If there are genuine mitigating factors then our partner will probably know them anyway. When we apply this principle the sub-text becomes: 'Regardless of the factors involved, our relationship is my priority issue. If I've caused you any hurt, I want to say sorry and make things right between us.'

In conclusion

Forgiveness is a much more complex topic than it at first appears, often more complicated than some preachers imply! What is perhaps the most important point to underline is that forgiveness is not an end in itself but a starting point: to restored relationships, to healing, to being the people God wants us to be.

Questions

1. Are there particular things for which you need to forgive your partner?

2. Are there particular things for which you ought to ask your partner's forgiveness?

3. Are you still carrying around hurts from your past that impact on the present? Is there anyone responsible for those hurts that you need to forgive?

4. How good are you at demonstrating that you've really forgiven your partner for something? What can you do to be better at this?

Hot Spots!

Point to ponder

Think about the disagreements in your marriage that (a) are the most heated and (b) keep recurring. What do the disagreements tend to be about?

In marriage counselling, there are a number of areas that can frequently be identified as the catalyst for serious problems in marriage: money, time and sex. It's not that these things themselves are necessarily problematic or difficult, but that these are things about which one or both partners may have a lot of powerful feelings and emotions. As a result, these areas can become either a serious battleground within a marriage or else are not talked about, because of the difficulties associated with the issues when they've been raised before. So the issues remain. A sudden crisis may bring them quickly to the fore; or worse, a stray spark sets them off, exploding all over the place in unpredictable ways. There may be casualties, there will almost certainly be injuries. What we need to do is resolve the foundational issues that led to the battle in the first place.

We'll look at each of these three topics in turn. It may be that you do not have difficulties with all or any of them. If so, don't look for problems that might not be there! Rather, work through the sections as a self-audit, the results of which can then be encouragements to you that these parts of your marriage are good and healthy. But if you sense that one or more of these topics are problems in your marriage, work through them with optimism. It is easier than you may think to address these matters in a constructive and effective way, once you have the willingness to look at the topics afresh with the appropriate communication tools. If one or more of these topics have led to serious battles in the past, then you and your partner may need to agree on a temporary truce so as to look at the topics together. Don't be content with the truce; it should be an opportunity to resolve the issues on a more permanent basis.

Money

In 1 Timothy 6:10 we are told that 'the love of money is the root of all sorts of evil' (or: 'all evils.') Why is this? If Scripture merely asked the question of what was the root of many evils, how many of us would come up with 'love of money' as the first answer? More likely, we would guess at things such as hatred, envy or pride. Interestingly, the statement isn't unique to Paul. We can find very similar statements in secular writers of the time. When both important secular philosophers and perhaps the greatest Christian theologian say the same thing, we can reasonably conclude that we are dealing with something that is not only a key part but also an obvious part of the essential human condition. This verse in 1 Timothy is often used in isolation. We are probably well aware that the popular version, 'money is the root of all evil', is not what Paul says and has no Scriptural authority. But we may be less aware of where the verse fits into the overall matter that is being dealt with in this section of chapter 6. Paul is talking about the importance of doctrine. The very word 'doctrine' may cause us to switch off, associating it with theory and apparently having little to do with day-to-day Christian living. Paul anticipates such an objection! He talks of the importance of the understanding of doctrine not remaining as mere knowledge but as a means of leading to godliness, which he considers a matter of great gain (vv. 3-6). It is at this point

Paul anticipates an unspoken objection: the implication is that developing such godliness, living the Christian life better, is costly, for it will take time and effort. And if we allocate time and effort to becoming more Christ-like then the implication is that we shall have less time and resources to devote to earning a living. The implicit answer Paul gives to this is to recognise the truth of the objection. His answer is not to try and compromise, to try to live schizophrenic lives, but to learn greater contentment with what we have. The combination of godliness and contentment is very powerful (v. 6). Jesus said much the same thing: 'No servant can serve two masters. Either he will hate the one and love the other, or he will be devoted to the one and despise the other. You cannot serve both God and Money' (Luke 16:13). It is against this background that Paul speaks of the love of money being the root of all sorts of evil. Why? Because it is a major obstacle to godliness and contentment.

The problem that we may have is not with the lack of desire for godliness but fears about how we can be content if we make godliness a priority over earning a living. And it's no use telling ourselves, or telling our partner, this shouldn't be so. The fears may not be right but they may be very real. The core issue is how we help one another to address those fears. To put it another way, how can we help one another to be content?

There are two important and related points that we can notice simply from experience and anecdotal evidence. Firstly, the truth of the old adage that money doesn't bring happiness. Theoretically we know that to be true; there are too many examples of very wealthy people being unhappy and discontented to doubt the veracity of the saying. Naturally we know the related jokes: such as 'Maybe, but money helps one to be miserable in comfort.' And it would be foolish to deny that such jokes contain some truth. But our quest here is not for comfort but contentment. Over recent years, there have been more and more examples of people giving up high-powered jobs with huge salaries, to live far more simple lives, perhaps running a smallholding on a Scottish island or a craft workshop in rural England. Such people are usually honest enough to report certain hardships but claim that their substantially increased contentment has made it worthwhile. The concept of 'downsizing' has become an accepted and positive thing to do, not a measure of failure. Secondly, we can easily notice, with only scant observation, that very few people love money for its own sake. To do so would be silly, for ultimately it's only pieces of paper, or these days, electronic figures in a computer. What people want are things that they perceive money can access: power and influence at the extreme end of the spectrum, but, more commonly, things such as security, peace of mind, opportunities for the children, and suchlike. Unless we came from wealthy backgrounds, most of us can remembering the agony of wondering how we were going to meet an essential bill, contrasted with the satisfaction of being financially much better off and being able to pay similar bills without major anxiety, usually in later life.

One other factor that we must inevitably take into account is that those of us in the West live in a very materialistic society. In post-war society, a refrigerator was often perceived by many as a luxury and television some form of distant dream. Most newly-marrieds would naturally expect to make do with secondhand furniture and live in rented accommodation while they saved up. Cars were, if not exceptional, hardly the norm. What a previous generation thought of as luxuries, we consider necessities. A mortgaged home without a fridge-freezer, microwave, at least one television and recent model car would be thought of as exceptional and probably deprived. VCRs or DVDs, PCs and satellite TV are part of everyday life. Whereas the post-war generation expected to pass children's clothes on from child to child, now expensive designer clothing for children is frequently perceived as loving parenting. Our list of essentials grows as our list of what we can do without shrinks. Even if we can't afford some or all of these things, our expectation is that we *should* be able to. There is a sense of injustice if we have to do without.

The cost of all this is money upfront, or increased debt. This has to be earned, often at the cost of a taxing job (or jobs) with longer hours and bigger fears about losing one's job. The requirement of a husband and wife both earning may in itself necessitate some of the extra outgoings on such things as child-minders and more expensive instant meals.

At this point, it may appear that we are about to suggest the importance of taking a fresh look at our lifestyle expectations, with the answer being to develop a less materialistic attitude. That's not our intention, although that is not to imply such a life-style review wouldn't be helpful. (We'll think about that a bit more when we come to discuss time.) The main focus of this section is money and how our attitude towards it impacts on our marriage, not materialism *per se*.

The major problem and its root cause

The major problem associated with money in marriage is easy to define: it is where the partners have different attitudes towards money issues. At its most extreme, this is when each has a conflicting attitude. This is almost always the root reason for the battle, resulting in bombardments typified by the accusation mortar: 'You shouldn't think like that!' Although the conflicting attitudes may be the reason for the battle, it's not the root cause. For that we have to dig a little deeper and find out not only what our partner thinks but feels. That requires sensitivity and understanding, two commodities always in short supply in the midst of the battle. That's why a truce is the necessary first step. As an example of getting to the root cause, let's consider this hypothetical situation.

The husband had grown up in a family where, for whatever reason, money was always short. He has many childhood memories of his parents arguing about money: his mother blaming his father for not getting a better paid job, and his father accusing his mother of not managing the household expenses effectively. Money for school trips might have been paid but was often accompanied by guilt-inducing statements such as 'I can't really afford to give you this but I'll go without lunch for a cou-ple of days.' Unexpected expenses, such as the old car breaking down again, would cast a blanket of depression and anxiety over the household for days, with the parents arguing more than usual. Pleas for special trips to places such as the funfair would have to be made hesitantly, with expectations of disappointment and being told 'We can't afford it.' It was made clear to him that 'he should learn to be good with money so as not to be like his father!' The message was always delivered with emotional force rather than constructive love. He received no careful guidance from his parents on how to handle money and he had no helpful role models. His teenage years were full of complaints about how much he was costing, growing out of things quickly and school clothes being so expensive. His perception of his parents' longed for future was when he left school and could go out to work. The message about going to college or university was: 'Well, of course if you really want to go, we'll manage somehow.' Consequently, early on in his childhood he began to form the conclusion: 'Lack of money is the cause of family unhappiness. More money equals less rows.' The boy determined at least two things: firstly that when he grew up he would put a lot of effort into having money so his wife would love him and secondly, that money should be a topic which was avoided in his adult household because it was an unpleasant and uncomfortable subject. Deep in his subconscious a default setting was created based on these childhood conclusions.

The wife's childhood experiences were different. While her family was perhaps a bit better off financially, her parents were excellent money managers. They had regular discussions about financial issues. If they were unable to afford something, this would be a joint decision and never a source of conflict. In times of hardship, cheerfulness was the order of the day, making a family trip to the park a great occasion, even though a more expensive trip out had been the original hope. The girl's mother and father had always explained to her what was and wasn't possible financially and why. She was actively encouraged to develop good money habits. In teenage years she knew her parents were saving and planning for her future, whether that was higher education, marriage or something else entirely.

From an early age, she both observed and experienced that money was simply a tool within family life. For her it had no direct connection with happiness or unhappiness. It was merely something to be managed and clearly discussed, without major emotions being attached to it. Of course there would be times of regret and perhaps even hardship but these could be got through together. Other, less costly, substitutes could always be found.

When the young couple meet and start going out together, the man probably finds that his future wife's attitude towards money is one of the things that is attractive about her. Of course, at the early stages of their relationship their money is still totally separate so there is little incentive to discuss it. Even when their relationship gets more serious, the woman may see no need to discuss financial issues, as she assumes that their financial strategy will be much the same as her parents'. By contrast, the man will, probably without his future wife even noticing, take this opportunity of establishing what for him is an important principle in their relationship: to avoid the topic of money. Why? Because he associates such discussion with arguments and unhappiness and he wants their relationship to be free of both.

Once married, they begin to experience financial problems. One reason is that the husband decides to take responsibility for the household finances but his money management skills are poor. At first, his wife doesn't particularly notice because it's not the sort of thing she is looking for. She's surprised that they don't talk about money but it's not a major concern for her at this point. She assumes a pattern will settle down to her more familiar norm once they've been married a bit longer. It is only when a financial crisis hits that she becomes alert to the problems. She tries to talk to her husband but he rebuffs such attempts. It's an area where he feels both uncomfortable and a failure so defaults to avoiding it. She feels hurt and powerless. As the financial problems grow she becomes more and more desperate, pleading emotionally and powerfully for her husband to talk to her. He does so only in the most limited fashion, with his emotions on red alert. She feels alienated, and unable to use her much better financial management skills. Her hurt is communicated as accusation. His strategy is to try and ignore the problem as much as possible but one of his childhood default principles comes to the fore: he must earn more money. If he can earn more money then they will be better off and their unhappiness will go away. So he works harder and longer, is away from home more and his wife feels more and more alone and rejected. She begins to accuse him of caring more about his job than her. Even though he has always intended not to do so, the same climate that he hated in his parents' household has been reproduced, albeit in a subtly different form.

Although the above example is obviously stylised, such situations are far from uncommon. What can be done? What follows are steps that can be taken. The order is not set in stone and may need to be adjusted to take into account your own situation.

Step 1

What is perfectly obvious when we read this case study is that our hypothetical couple need to talk about the situation. The real question is how? The husband's default setting is to avoid talking about the issue; his wife has no experience of raising the topic with someone who doesn't want to talk about it. The reality is that she is the one who has to find an approach that works. Analytically, her problem is that while her natural approach may be emotional exasperation with him for not talking about the issues, any hint of emotion is likely to drive him further and further behind his default barriers. Thus the most effective approach is likely to be gentle and unemotional, beginning with coaxing him away from his barriers. The immediate problems and potential solutions about financial management need to be put to one side. The starting point is an exposure and examination of each other's default settings. This must be done with extreme sensitivity and love. The first aim is not to judge each other's default settings but to understand and empathise with them. Here typical counselling questions will help.

Using our hypothetical couple, the wife should ask the husband:

- Tell me how you felt when you heard your parents rowing about money.
- Did you think your parents resented you because you were a financial burden?
- How old were you when [such and such] happened?
- With hindsight, how accurate do you think your assessment of the situation was?
- How would you summarise your views about finance in marriage? How do they look when you review them in the cold light of adulthood?
- What are your biggest fears about money?
- What would you like our joint strategy towards money to look like? How can I help bring this about?

Using the hypothetical couple again, the husband should ask the wife:

- What were the features about your childhood that made money a comfortable topic?
- What assumptions do you think you've made about financial issues as a result of your upbringing?
- What are your fears about our present situation?
- How do you think you can best help to establish a good approach to money in our relationship?

Step 2

Once a genuine, albeit preliminary, understanding has been reached, it is then possible to move on towards solutions. The next stage may be to cross-check how love is felt and communicated. If the husband's language of love here is all about giving, he may drive himself to work harder and longer hours to try and provide. If the wife's language of love here is about being together, she may be much happier and feel more loved if he is less involved in money generation so they can spend more time together.

Step 3

Below is a questionnaire that then can be used in two related ways: to summarise the discussion so far and to identify specific problem areas. The results can then be used to set an agenda for future discussion, which could be now or in the near future. To have got this far may be emotionally exhausting and, if either party is a natural problem solver, they may need to be prepared to postpone detailed solutions for a bit longer!

Against each of the following statements, indicate which of the following categories is, in your opinion, the most accurate:

- Strongly agree
- Generally agree
- Yes and no ...
- Disagree
- Strongly disagree

You will probably find it easiest to write the questions on separate sheets of paper and then write the answers in.

1. Overall, we have a healthy and Biblical approach to money issues.
2. I have still have emotional baggage/hang-ups about money from my experiences prior to marriage.
3. I worry about money issues.
4. I think my partner is too concerned about money and money issues.
5. I feel that we discuss money issues in an open and constructive manner.

6. Given the option, I'd prefer us to have less money but more time.
7. All our money (income, savings, *et cetera*) is jointly shared.
8. I believe that we give away an appropriate amount.
9. We plan our short-, medium- and long-term expenditure together.
10. Many of our disagreements are about money issues.
11. If we had more money we'd have far fewer problems.
12. I have some resentment about how my partner spends money.
13. I find it very uncomfortable to talk about money issues.

After you have both answered the questions above, go through your answers together. On the basis of all your answers, identify if there are issues about money that you need to discuss further. Some issues you may be able to discuss immediately, others may need more time. Decide together how you can best approach such a discussion in a non-threatening and constructive way. It may be helpful to focus on why your partner has answered in the way they have. Take into account your and your partner's answer to question 13.

The final step

This may need to come some time after the above stages. Draft an approach to financial issues that you can both buy into! The prompt questions below can be used as a basis for drafting such a strategy.

- Will we have formal and regular discussions about financial issues, such as monthly budgeting?
- If we have a budget, how strict will it be? The answer to this needs to take into account temperament and personality, as well as financial constraints.

- Will we only commit to a major purchase if we agree it in advance?
- How much can each person spend without agreeing the expenditure?
- What happens if one of us 'breaks the rules'?
- Who takes responsibility for what?
- What are our financial goals? Immediate, short-term, medium-term, long-term?
- If a financial matter arises and one of us needs to talk about it unexpectedly, would it be helpful to have some sort of warning signal or phrase that can be used? This means that the other person can respond: 'OK, now is as good a time as any to talk', or: 'I don't feel able to talk about it now because …'

Time

Time is perhaps the most common issue couples identify as a problem in marriage. However, when considering it as a problem we must be careful not to mistake the symptom for the cause. The problem is inseparably linked with many of the issues we've discussed in the chapter 'Who am I? Who are you?' and that is the backdrop to what we'll think about here.

The 168 Factor

168. One hundred and sixty-eight. No matter how we put it, it's a non-negotiable figure. It's the total number of hours in a week. Most of us find it a surprising number; shocking even, when we first think about it. Somehow it doesn't *feel* enough. Instinctively we believe a week should be longer. But it isn't. It's the same figure that our parents, grandparents and great-grandparents had to work with and the figure that our children, grandchildren and great-grandchildren will have to learn to cope with. But it gets worse: 168 is the gross figure. In practice we have to

work with a net figure, because no matter how time-efficient we learn to be, we all have to sleep. Of course, different people need different amounts of sleep. But we need to underline here that if we cut corners on sleep it is likely to be counter-productive, for we need an appropriate amount of sleep to function effectively. It's generally accepted that most people need about eight hours a night, which reduces the net hours available for our waking lives to 112.

Only in physics is there any value in talking about time being relative to the speed of light! In the everyday world, when clinically faced with the 168 figure, we accept with our heads that it is a non-negotiable. But not all of us really believe it! People whose personalities include a strong element of what we've called unstructured in the chapter 'What am I? What are you?' often have a sub-conscious belief that time too can be unstructured. That is why unstructured people are so often late for commitments: despite what the clock (or diary) may be telling them, they are optimistic they can squeeze in something else. Ironically, unstructured people are those who are least likely to use time management principles, so their attempt to fit something else into their schedule will frequently be done in a spontaneous and unscientific way. But with the 168 factor, structured people don't always fare any better. They can easily believe that if they are more structured, more effective in their organisation of time then they too can squeeze more things into the 168.

Can time management help?

Anyone involved in business has probably been exposed to some form of time management training. Complex personal organisers with lots of different inserts designed to help us make more effective use of our time are readily available. Browse any bookshop and self-help books on developing more time-effective habits are easy to find. Now certainly these things can help us be more effective in our use of time. But let's also be clear that simply buying an expensive time management tool, going on a time management course or reading a book on developing effective habits will not in itself make us more effective in our use of time. These things have to be lived out and our basic personality, particularly whether we're structured or unstructured, will either be a great help or a major block to that end. The truth is that highly structured people instinctively apply most of the basic principles of good time management. Long before they even knew of sophisticated systems and personal organisers, they were using simple diaries for more than just noting dates: keeping different lists of priorities and things to do, in their head planning how to minimise the time spent on shopping trips, and so forth. A formal time management system may be great for them, not as a starting point but an additional tool. By contrast, if unstructured people don't naturally make priority lists *et cetera*, formal time management training may wash over them, even if they think it is great in theory. They may accept the wisdom of doing things such as spending the last fifteen minutes of one working day identifying the priorities for the following day but not actually do anything about it.

People who are naturally structured frequently experience what we've come to call 'Boxer syndrome'. In his brilliant 'Fairy story for adults', *Animal Farm*, George Orwell describes a shire house called Boxer. He is the reliable stalwart of the animals' revolution against the oppressive farmers. Although not one of the leaders of the revolution, he is a great supporter and constantly uses his great strength and determination for the benefit of the other animals and the revolution – not that he would ever make such a distinction. Whenever the leaders' plans get into trouble and projects fall behind schedule, Boxer sets his alarm to get up even earlier for work. His great motto, which inspires all the other animals, is 'I must work harder.' And work harder and harder he does. Despite his great strength he eventually drives himself into the ground. He comes to a literally sticky end, as his only worth to the leaders at this point is to be sent off to the glue factory. Highly structured people's approach to the 168 factor is to adopt Boxer's motto or a variation of it and decide they must work harder. They may achieve a great deal in terms of task accomplishment but the cost to themselves or their families may be high. If they have a need to find their self-image in either relationships or achievement, then they will often aim to do more than is reasonably possible, either to gain the approval of others or to gain a sense of achievement.

Unstructured people have a different motto, along the lines of 'I must get around to …' One main pitfall they have to watch out for is reacting to other people's agendas and priorities rather than focusing on their own. This is a particular danger if their self-image is based on approval and in this sense they run very similar risks to their structured counterpart. If their self-image is based on achievement, the unstructured person may find themselves increasingly frustrated as time to devote to their own tasks keeps getting lost. Often they will be last-minute people, motivated by deadlines.

Combining strengths; minimising weaknesses

In a marriage context it is good to be aware of how each other's personalities impact on our approach to time. If the personality types with regard to structure are close or similar, then there will probably be harmony in approach to time. The problems arise when one partner is fairly or highly structured, and the other is fairly or highly unstructured. However, with mutual understanding and support, they can combine each other's natural strengths to make an effective whole. As always, the starting point is genuine understanding rather than 'I wish you would learn to …' type accusations.

Helpful hints where one partner is structured and the other is unstructured:

• Both need to recognise that change is not easy

A highly structured person will not easily appreciate that things such as making lists of daily priorities may require a huge amount of emotional effort from their unstructured partner. And an unstructured person will not find it easy to understand the high levels of anxiety a structured person will experience if asked to operate without lists and structures.

• Who keeps the diary?

Although both unstructured and structured people can have a similar difficulty in saying 'no' to external things, a structured person can find it easier to communicate a 'no'. The reason is that they already have things listed and can, quite legitimately, say things such as 'I'm sorry, we've already got something on that evening.' The unstructured person will not necessarily be deterred by something being in the diary! Their natural perception is that it's probably possible to do both things, even if logically it involves being in two places at the same time. So a good rule of thumb is to agree that the unstructured partner makes a point of leaving the acceptance or declining of invitations to the structured partner. Although it may feel slightly awkward at first, it is actually reasonable to respond to a request with the statement 'My wife/husband is in charge of the diary; I'll need to check with them first.' Of course it is important not to use the other partner as an excuse, with comments such as 'Well I would have liked to but he/she wouldn't agree.'

• Unstructured lists!

Lists are the natural, liberating tool of the structured person but they can look intimidating and restricting to their unstructured partner. One option is to create opportunities for unstructured lists. This can be somewhere where the unstructured partner can jot something down when it occurs to them, rather than being expected to contribute to a formal list discussion. Sticky notes at strategic points around the house, or paper stuck on the fridge door, are examples. The structured partner then takes responsibility for monitoring these and incorporating them into their more formal lists.

- Agreeing a strategy for punctuality

Unstructured people are very often late for appointments. Structured partners may adopt a strategy of giving their partner an earlier time as a way of ensuring they are ready. Although this is understandable, it is risky. For one thing, we should be aware that although well intentioned, it is a form of lying. It may make the marriage work better but is a dangerous precedent. The partner may also resent being told a false time. Getting to an event on time may be less important than arriving there in good spirits. On a practical note, the unstructured partner will quickly learn and assume that 7.30 really means 8.00. What really needs to happen is agreeing a strategy well in advance. This may include the unstructured person giving their partner permission to nag them at appropriate points well in advance of the getting ready stage; and firmly, but sensitively, to veto things that may over-run into getting ready time. As with so many things, the time to discuss strategy is not when the issue is immediate, but well in advance of the actual situation.

- Ensure humour is part of what goes on

Humour can be a far more effective tool than aggression. Joking about each other's tendencies can be very good, providing the humour is appropriate and supportive. Pointing at a big clock with a rueful smile may communicate more effectively than a harsh 'Do you realise what time it is?' Visual reminders, providing they don't become weapons, can be effective because they offer an opportunity for the other person to respond to the situation rather than having to deal with judgemental comments. In other words, they are empowering because they warn the person that there is a matter that requires active response but gives them the freedom to choose how. It is treating them as an adult rather than as a child.

Planning the future, living in the present

Although we've never been able to confirm its truth, we understand that in the Australian outback there are signs that warn
drivers: 'Choose your rut carefully. You'll be in it for the next
300 miles.' When it comes to how we use our time, many of us
find ourselves in the equivalent of a deep rut that we cannot
easily escape. Frequently one partner – often the husband,
although not always, – is in a job that requires them to work long
hours, far more than the traditional 9 to 5. Add on bringing
work home in the evening and at weekends, plus time spent
commuting and work seems to dominate most of the person's
waking hours. If both partners are in such jobs they may be
building up relationship problems by not seeing enough of each
other. However, the more common situation is where one partner, usually the wife, feels her husband neglects her for his job.
Work seems to be given a much higher priority and the wife
may feel taken for granted. This will often lead to accusations
such as 'I obviously don't matter to you'; 'You're always at
work'; 'Where do I feature on your list of priorities?' Such accusations may accurately reflect how the wife feels, but may not
reflect reality, because men don't usually think in such terms.
Men tend to compartmentalise more than women and how they
allocate their time and energies is seldom an accurate indicator
of their priorities. It is a gender difference that women may not
immediately understand. But even if pressure of work is identified and agreed as being a problem, there is often a sense of
being powerless. One partner may say: 'I know it's a problem
but I can't do anything about it. It's impossible to make changes
at the moment.' Although this appears to be an analytical
assessment, it's really a feelings statement. Many people who
feel that their company can't manage without them get, quite
literally, a shock when they suddenly find themselves being
made redundant. The reality is change is always possible but
it may not be either easy or comfortable. The principle is to have
a strategy to which both partners want to be committed. We
can arrive at such a strategy by again working through some

steps. In the first instance it is preferable to do this exercise individually, without direct consultation with each other.

Step 1: A time audit (or, life is a pie)

Forget detailed time logs; a back-of-the-envelope approach is perfectly adequate. Indeed, it's better to work with quick gut reaction responses here than to attempt scientific ones.

(a) Draw a circle. Freehand will do, no marks for expert geometry! This represents an average snapshot of your life. Decide what period you need to use to get a meaningful snapshot, in mathematical terms, an average. Depending on your situation, this may be a week, a month or perhaps a term.

(b) Summarise your life in four to six categories. (six is the maximum allowed by the exercise.) It's entirely up to you what categories you use but some typical ones are:

- work: whether this is paid work, work in the home, or whatever.
- church: this might be sub-divided into personal spirituality and corporate spirituality or, possibly more honestly, time with God and church events.
- partner: time just with each other.
- family: children, extended family.
- self: this might include individual leisure, personal development.

(c) Put these four to six categories on the circle to create a pie chart. It may look something like the example on the next page.

(d) Structured people and possibly some unstructured people, will be wondering whether issues such as sleep, eating, going to the bathroom, *et cetera* are included in self? No. Ignore these things altogether.

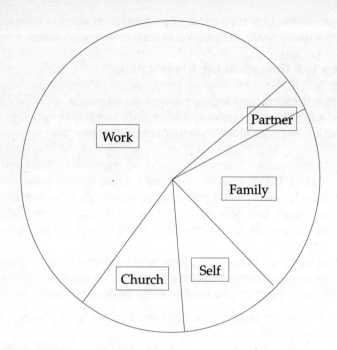

Step 2: Reflect

When you're satisfied that your pie chart gives a reasonable reflection of how you spend your time, the next thing is to ask yourself if you're happy with what you see. Is this what you want your life to look like?

Step 3: Dream

If you're genuinely content with what you see, then that's the last step in the exercise for you. However, most people find that ideally they'd like to make some changes.

(a) Redraw the pie chart, preferably using the same categories, although it's not against any rules to change them if you really wish, to reflect your dream. Note: dream, not fantasy. Fantasy is, for example, suddenly being left millions of pounds by a long-lost aunt so you don't ever have to work again. Dream is to work for a comfortable proportion of your time so that it doesn't exclude other priorities. It may change to look something like this:

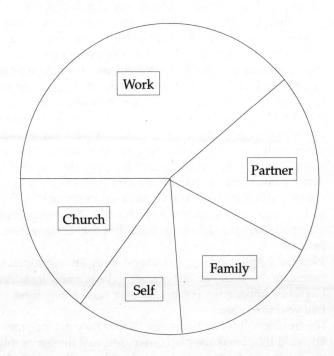

(b) Deliberately put to one side for the moment pessimistic statements such as 'But it isn't possible in the real world.'

Step 4: Share your dream and dream together

(a) At this point it may be helpful to share your result with your partner. In counselling situations this alone has often been liberating to some wives. It helps them to see that their husband's dream isn't to spend more and more time at work or at the golf club and, therefore, away from them. Having said that, this is not the main aim of the exercise. Neither is the main aim to implement the dream, although that is part of the purpose.

(b) Discuss and, if necessary, sensitively debate the dream/s It's at this point that the main aim emerges: to have made a conscious decision to buy into a dream together; to have chosen the rut carefully and to have chosen it together.

(c) Count the cost. Recognise that the dream may have a price tag, perhaps a big one. In reality it may not be possible for the main earning partner to work less hours in their present job. Simply going to one's line manager and announcing that you're only going to work a 35 hour week rather than the 60 hour week that has become the norm may just not be feasible; or if it is, future promotions may not happen. It may be necessary to change jobs and perhaps learn to be content with a less well paid but also less exacting role. This in turn may mean other major changes. The temptation may be to put the dream on hold. But that is dangerous. Instead:

(d) Plan an implementation strategy with an appropriate timescale. We'd all like our dreams to be possible instantly but that's unrealistic. The dream may need a two, three or five year timescale.

(e) The trouble with long timescales is that they get forgotten. To avoid this, break the plan down into, say, three monthly segments and diarise reviews. Such a plan will naturally be more detailed at the beginning and vaguer towards the end and it will need to be adjusted from time to time. The first couple of segments may include something like this:

Months 0–3

- Regularly pray about dream time structure and revise accordingly.

- Share your thinking with trusted friends and pastoral leaders.
- Make a list of possible consequences of doing nothing.
- Do preliminary research on possible changes such as job and house.

Months 4–6

- Start sending for details of other jobs.
- Update CV.
- Find articles about people who have made major changes to life and evaluate possible lessons.
- Book annual leave at time that is suitable for family rather than job.

To state the blatantly obvious, simply drawing up a couple of pie charts and an implementation strategy will not in itself make a difference. Their real value is to act as a catalyst for discussion and a commitment to buy in to the costs and benefits together. Even if the eventual conclusion is that, despite all the problems, the present time balance is the least worst option, the benefit is that it is a conscious and joint choice.

Sex

It's not our intention here to offer a comprehensive Christian guide to sex. What we aim to do is to highlight some areas of potential misunderstanding and conflict, look at some common problems and consider some issues, in order to enable couples to overcome obstacles in the way of a healthy and Biblical approach to lovemaking. Many problems that appear to be sexual problems in a marriage often have their roots in misunderstandings about a partner's sexuality, an ignorance of the gender effect or some unresolved conflict from the past. Often, simply having a greater knowledge and understanding of these issues and how they can impact on the relationship can empower couples to make any necessary adjustments. Using the communication tools previously discussed, couples can begin to talk openly about problems.

Sexual love sets marriage apart from all other relationships. It is the only relationship where sexual intercourse, love-making, is allowed. Unless disease or disability prevents it, lovemaking can be expected to be an integral part of marriage until death. Abraham and Sarah, for instance, were still making love well past the time of Sarah's menopause and when she herself had no expectation of having children. But for many reasons, not all couples enjoy making love as much as they could. Indeed, what should be a time of great intimacy can sometimes become either a battleground or a no-go area.

Secular society has hijacked sex. What God created as pure and beautiful has become corrupted into an unclean industry. Consequently, we may believe that not talking about love-making to our partner, being ultra-modest, possibly even coy, in our attitude to sex is the 'right' Christian attitude. But some of our reticence may actually be cultural. Some cultures are very open about sex, others are much more reserved. Each attitude has its problems but the important thing is to recognise our own cultural bias and not automatically equate it with being Biblical. An incomplete or mistaken perception of the Biblical view of sex is just one of the things that can mar our lovemaking.

Some others are:

- A lack of understanding of the way gender affects our own and our partner's sexuality
- Past abuse
- Past painful experiences, both physical and mental
- Unresolved issues in the relationship
- Medical problems
- Emotional problems
- An imperfect knowledge of our partner's sexuality
- An incomplete knowledge of our own sexuality
- Difficulties in talking about sex with our partner

Pause and Reflect

Read Song of Songs Chapter 7. Christians interpret this book in different ways; but however the text is interpreted the fact remains that explicit erotic images are used. There is no doubt about the depth of feeling between the man and woman in the song.

- To what extent do you think it is acceptable for couples to share their sexual fantasies?
- Should couples dress in clothing which has sexual appeal for their partner?
- On what do you base your answers?

Some physical problems have their roots in early married life

Some Christians have high expectations of their honeymoon. They eagerly look forward to experiencing great mutual delight in their lovemaking, especially if they have practised restraint during their courtship. For some this is indeed a time of great bliss, but for other couples it can be a time of real difficulty.

- Their first experience of lovemaking may fall far short of their expectations.
- One partner may be perfectly happy about their physical love but the other partner may be unsatisfied.
- One or both may be totally ignorant of practical techniques.
- They may have difficulty 'fitting the bits together'.

A particular problem has been known to occur if a couple have lived together or made love with one another before marriage. Their sex life may have been perfectly satisfactory before marriage but suddenly, once they are married, it becomes less so. There can be a variety of reasons why this happens but the first step in tackling the problem should be to pray about the situation and go through a stage of repentance. Once forgiveness has been sought, any specific difficulties can then be tackled. Most early problems disappear with time. Familiarity with our partner's body and an awareness of our own sexuality, experimenting with techniques, being less shy and more comfortable with one another, all help to develop lovemaking that is satisfying for both partners. But in a few cases this is not so. Early problems or disappointments are found to persist and if one or both partners continues to be dissatisfied by their lovemaking, they may not feel able to own up to this. The partner may bury their concerns, hoping they will go away. Problems not tackled early on can have a long-term detrimental effect on the marriage. The good news is that it is never too late to start putting things right. Communication, talking and praying about the issue, possibly seeking advice or reading relevant Christian books are all helpful courses of action.

Case study

Jayne and Bill have been married for three years. Both are Christians, from Christian families. After what seemed to be a reasonably good honeymoon, their lovemaking settled down into a satisfactory state but now they hardly ever make love at all. Both are aware that this is not a good state to be in.

Bill was brought up to respect women and believes that he should not be 'making demands' on his wife. He is a thoughtful, analytical person, kind and caring. He is easily hurt and is terrified of getting himself into a situation where Jayne might reject him. Secretly, he longs for Jayne sometimes to take charge of their lovemaking sessions so that he will be in no danger of being rejected.

Jayne is an outgoing, lively woman. As a teenager she enjoyed reading romantic fiction. She enjoys old films of the swashbuckling type, where the hero risks all to rescue the woman of his dreams and ends by making passionate love to her. Secretly, she longs for Bill to be so overcome by desire for her that he picks her up in his arms and sweeps her away to bed to make passionate love.

1. *Is Bill's fantasy of having Jayne take charge of lovemaking reasonable? If not, why not? Is it likely to just start happening? What could Bill do for his fantasy to become reality?*

2. *Is Jayne's fantasy of being swept off her feet and into bed reasonable? If not, why not? Is it likely to spontaneously occur? What could Jayne do to make it more likely? Bill is very shy of talking about sex. Is there a way they can communicate without talking or anything else either of them can do to improve the situation?*

How gender effect can affect our sexuality

In most cases, sexuality is strongly linked to gender. But it is important to emphasise that we are thinking here in general terms based on common, but not inflexible, patterns. This is quite different from stereotyping people according to gender and there are many exceptions to every case.

Usually, men are easily aroused. Perfume, touch, attractive clothing, talk about sex, provocative images, an attractive woman, can all trigger the male hormone testosterone. This powerful chemical is designed to produce the response: 'Ready for action! – Now!' Once triggered, it usually takes time and effort for a man to return his libido to the 'off' or even 'standby' stage. If a man is very aroused, not making love at this point can lead to intense frustration, sometimes even emotional or physical misery. Most women and many men have an understanding of the premenstrual tension effect of female hormones on women at certain times of the month, but many wives do not understand the powerful effect the hormone testosterone can have on men. Often, when a husband wants to make love to his wife he has a real driving need. A wife can sometimes be puzzled and upset by this need, especially when she is tired. She can interpret his need as an unreasonable demand, as his being unloving or unfeeling. She may not realise how hurt and rejected her husband may feel when she refuses. A man's ego is usually at its most fragile and he can be at his most vulnerable around the whole aspect of making love. This does not, of course, mean that a woman has to give in to her husband; rather that she should be gentle and sensitive in her refusal.

Helpful Hint

It is useful for couples to agree together in advance of bed-time whether or not they will be making love. That way, a husband will not be faced with last minute rejection and a wife will not have to cope with being the one to say 'no'. It can also act as a prelude to making love.

On the whole, men are aroused much quicker than women. This difference has been likened to the difference between a modern, gas barbecue which only takes a few minutes to heat up and be ready for action, and the old-fashioned charcoal type that has to be lit an hour before it's needed. Women generally need more time to be ready for sex, they need time to be aroused and fully stimulated to participate in lovemaking. Below are some examples of things that have all been known to arouse women:

- Being paid attention, being listened to, having eye contact when talking
- A romantic gesture
- A planned romantic interlude
- Having neck, arms, other 'non-sexual' areas kissed and caressed
- A favourite after-shave
- Fresh male sweat
- Being swept off her feet by a passionate husband
- A husband taking the trouble to shower or shave before love-making
- Her husband's naked body

A display of real passionate desire, at an appropriate time and place, can be a powerful aphrodisiac for men and women alike.

> ### *Pause and Reflect*
>
> What things first aroused your desire for your partner?
> What things can your partner do to arouse you?

A common misunderstanding

If a wife refuses his sexual advances a husband can sometimes think 'she doesn't really love me', or, 'she's frigid!' or 'manipulative', or even 'calculating'. What many husbands do not understand is just how much most wives' sexuality is focused around their relationship, and how much a wife's desire to make love, or otherwise, is affected by her emotions. Wives need to *feel* loved in order to enter wholeheartedly into lovemaking. Women thrive on affection, attention, romance, being secure in the relationship, being made to feel at the centre of their husband's lives. Husbands often say: 'Of course I love my wife! She should know that!' Knowing objectively is not enough for a woman. Women need to *feel* loved. It can be as difficult for husbands to understand this as it can be for wives to understand the power of testosterone.

> ### *Pause and Reflect*
>
> In Genesis 3:16 God says to the woman, 'Your desire will be for your husband.'
>
> 1. As a husband, how can you increase your wife's desire for you?
> 2. As a wife, what can your husband do to increase your desire for him? What can you do to increase your desire for your husband?

If a husband doesn't want to make the effort to make his wife feel loved, she may not want to make the effort to make love; not as some form of punishment or sanction but a logical consequence. An important principle to note: *Many husbands need to make love to feel loving. Many wives need to feel loved to make love.*

I'm too tired!

'How can she say she's too tired?' is a question that some husbands have asked about their wives, sometimes adding, 'All she's got to do is to be there! What's tiring about that?' From the wife's perspective, perceiving that she is ignored all evening in favour of the TV, computer or other interest, and then once in bed, being faced with a husband wanting to make love is an almost guaranteed turn-off. Many women, especially when the children are very young, have long, demanding days. For the partner who is at home with children, the day can be particularly stressful. Being in charge of young children means being totally responsible for them 24 hours a day. Women do not have the monopoly on being too tired to make love. Men can also be too tired really to make love to their wives, settling instead for just sex. Just having sex may be fine sometimes, but healthy marriages need genuine lovemaking in order to thrive, unless there are good reasons why this is not possible. Most men can experience real pleasure from sex as a quick 'PS' at the end of the day but few women have the same facility. Women are just not made that way. A wife may get a physical 'buzz', and the experience may, to some extent, be satisfying, but all too often she can be left feeling unsatisfied, maybe even resentful. Of course, many wives do actively participate in last minute lovemaking. Even at the end of busy day when many demands have been made on a wife, she may still welcome sex. At this point a husband needs to be very sensitive to his wife's needs. Wives have been known to complain that during late night lovemaking they can be at a state of real arousal, looking forward to a satisfying climax, only to have the husband give a sudden happy sigh, roll over, and go to sleep. The wife is then left to cope with *her* hormones flooding around making her feel miserable, frustrated, unsatisfied, possibly resentful. An experience like this may make a wife very cautious about the circumstances under which she will make love in the future.

Pause and Reflect

If one of you is always too tired to make love, and has been over a long period of time, why is that? Does your lifestyle need overhauling? Is there a medical reason: a lack of iron; vitamins or not enough exercise? If you are married to someone who is always extremely tired, and you're not, are you taking your fair share of responsibility for domestic chores and childcare, *et cetera*?

Some effects of emotions

For both partners unresolved conflict, hurt or resentment can all inhibit lovemaking. For a man, making love can be a way to be reconciled after an argument. For women this is rarely so. Most wives will not recognise an attempt to make love after an argument as an attempt at reconciliation. They may view this as a total disregard of their feelings and may greet any sexual overtures very unsympathetically, possibly with some hostility. Wives need to recognise that for a husband, physical love may be his way of saying sorry. This does not, of course, mean that a wife is obliged to make love at this point as a way of demonstrating reconciliation! What it does mean that a wife might interpret a physical overture not as just sex but an attempt at reconciliation. Thus alerted, she is then in a better position to respond sensitively. Similarly, husbands need to understand that even if their wives do make love after an argument, they will probably still have a need to talk about the issue. Women almost always need to talk through issues in order to resolve them; strong emotions are hugely difficult for a woman to ignore, or 'put behind her'. Sexual activity does not necessarily draw a line under a previous problem.

Regular changes!

An added complication to lovemaking can be the fact that women's bodies follow a monthly cycle which can impact on their libido. At certain times of the month the libido is high and women are very interested in making love. At other times they are fairly interested, but there are times when women are actively disinterested, not wanting to be involved in sex at all. Some women are strongly cyclical; others are only mildly cyclical and hardly notice this effect; most are somewhere in between. A woman's body can also change during the course of the month. The position of the clitoris and the shape of the vagina may alter very slightly. Ways in which husbands touch their wives, which give great pleasure and are very arousing at one time of the month, may be totally unsuccessful or even unpleasant at another. If this happens, it is important for a wife not to pull away impatiently, or in any way make her husband feel rejected. It's not his fault! In the same way, a husband needs to understand that unexpected reactions to his attentions are not his wife being difficult; maybe it's just the way women are made!

Men are also cyclical, but their cycle generally follows the seasons. In general, men feel less sexual during the winter and much more sexual as spring approaches. Men can also experience a lessening or even loss of libido due to extreme tiredness, stress, lack of physical fitness or emotional problems. Many men experience a time of temporary impotence, because of a variety of factors, stress being perhaps the most common. Difficulty in maintaining an erection during lovemaking can be a problem for some men. If this problem persists, it should not be ignored. Help and advice are available for the majority of these kinds of problems. Issues such as these can be more of a problem into the 'third age'. Reliable testimony from many couples suggests that age alone should not be a barrier to the physical joy that God intends us to have in each other.

As Christians, God expects us to minister to one another. Unlike the world's view of sex, where both participants are often asking 'what's in it for me?' the Christian response is: 'how can I meet my partner's needs? How can I minister to my wife/ husband?' Lovemaking is a precious gift from God which He wants us to enjoy, and is a unique way for husbands and wives to minister to one another.

Hints for avoiding problems

- Communicate! Talking about sex can be difficult so find a time when you're both relaxed.
- Don't try and talk about issues just as you're about to make love. Set a time when you won't be interrupted and when there are no time pressures.
- Be as unemotional and analytical as you can. Use appropriate communication techniques to help discuss potentially difficult areas.
- Use non-verbal communication whilst making love to make your needs known to one another.
- Pray for one another. God answers prayer about our sex life as much He does about all other aspects of our marriage.

Questions

1. Are there issues about your own sexuality that you need to consider in more detail?

2. Are there issues about your partner's sexuality that it would be helpful for your relationship to discuss – sensitively?

3. Do you think your lovemaking has got into a rut? What steps can you take to make it better?

4. Are there any particular fears or concerns you have about lovemaking that it would be helpful for you to discuss with your partner? How can they help you to discuss the issues in a supportive and understanding way?

Not Being Content with Good Intentions

There are two final, serious but subtle obstacles that we need to consider: obstacles that can get in the way of your marriage becoming great. The first is the little voice that whispers: 'All this is very well, but my marriage can't really change. We're too set in our ways.' The best way to deal with this pessimistic whisper is to confront it straight on. Change happens to the apparently unchangeable all the time. A little fairy story:

> A community of caterpillars spend their days happily munching leaves on their home tree. Life is okay. But a rumour reaches the community that caterpillars can fly. Different caterpillars have different reactions. Some are cynical; some are excited; some are unsure; some say it's a nice idea but just not realistic. An enthusiastic caterpillar declares that what's needed is faith. He climbs to the end of the highest branch. He starts to flap his many legs as quickly as possible and leaps into space with hope in his heart. The others watch as he crashes to the ground. Fortunately, his fall is into soft grass and he survives, with only caterpillar bruises to show for his efforts. Hours later, he manages to crawl back up the tree, apparently older and wiser, convinced that although flight is a lovely dream it could never happen in his life. He's tried it but it hasn't worked. Later, looking up from his resigned munching, he sees a beautiful butterfly flap graciously past. He briefly envies the butterfly its flight, noting sadly that unlike the butterfly he hasn't got any wings. Mindful of the bruises, he determines never to try flying again.

Those of us who are not biologists talk too glibly about cater-
pillars turning into butterflies. Biologists know the incredible
biochemical and other changes it involves. The emergence of
the butterfly from the chrysalis involves considerable struggle
and takes place slowly. The caterpillar doesn't take a nap in
the sun and wake up to find itself a butterfly. To read the
New Testament is to read of God-empowered change. We are
promised it's possible and worthwhile; we are given no promises it will be easy. And while some God-empowered change
can be sudden, much is gradual. This leads us to the second of
our subtle obstacles.

The danger is we can be content with good intentions. It is no
accident that some of the most challenging words spoken by
Jesus come at the conclusion of the sermon on the mount:
'Therefore everyone who hears these words of mine, *and acts
upon them*, may be compared to a wise man, who built his house
upon the rock ...' (Matthew 7:24). Good intentions are good.
But they are no good if they are not put into practice. One way
of getting started is to plan some first-step changes in your life.
It's ideal if both partners can commit to this but if that is not
possible at the moment, God can still empower one partner
acting alone. The action planning should be related to specific
areas that the couple, or each individual, has identified as
important. It is usually easier for each partner to make
individual action plans.

The best action planning complies with certain principles and
each point should be:

• Realistic
• Observable (or capable of being observed)
• Measurable
• Have a time factor

So, for example, 'I will be a better husband/wife' is a poor
objective because it is too general, even though it may rest on
the best of intentions. Much better, although less spectacular,
is: 'I will put the rubbish out every day rather than wait for my

partner to do it.' (Because this is something I know my partner really hates and I can demonstrate *agape* love to them by putting out the rubbish myself.) Some people find the thumb-rule test borrowed from childhood of: 'Hey Dad, watch me …' helpful. 'Hey Dad, watch me be a better husband/wife' is difficult, what is there to see? But 'Hey Dad, watch me put the rubbish out every night' can be seen very clearly.

It's helpful if action planning is structured around the framework of one specific objective per period. Too many objectives, and we tend to fail and this can lead to discouragement. We recommend identifying:

- One thing I can do daily
- One thing I can do weekly
- One thing I can do monthly
- One thing I can do annually

Finally, some related 'health warnings'

1. Objectives can be joint but this can be more difficult in practice. So while the following objective may be good in itself: 'We will have a time of prayer together at least once a week', it's better to construct it as an individual objective: 'I will organise a joint time of prayer at least once per week'. This distinction is especially important where one partner perceives that the other does not take responsibility for things.
2. If both partners make objectives, it's usually helpful to share them with one another. However, it may be appropriate to keep at least some secret. For example, if your annual objective is: 'I will plan a surprise birthday party for my partner', it will be counter-productive to declare the objective in advance!
3. Objectives should never be used as weapons but as encouragement!
4. Action planning is not ideally suited for addressing serious problems.

Will good objectives transform your marriage? Not in themselves. Far more important is working through the core topics discussed in this book. That will take time and effort, not forgetting prayer. It will involve some stumbles, so it is important to give yourself permission to make mistakes. Falling off is part of learning to ride. What objectives will do is get you started. Don't worry if change seems like a long haul. In Acts chapter 10 Peter wrestles with God about some important change in his life. The change is necessary so Peter can begin to preach to non-Jews for the first time. The passage leaves us in no doubt the mission was a difficult one for Peter to cope with. He prepares what appears to be a long sermon. But God acts before Peter finishes (verse 44). What God required of Peter was a willingness to begin.

Epilogue

At the beginning of this book we speak of the divorce that never was. We make no secret that we are in marriage ministry because our own marriage so nearly ended in divorce. It is the memories of what went wrong for us, coupled with the testimony that God can heal and restore, that motivate us to stimulate others to live out Biblical principles in marriage.

Many people have encouraged us to tell the story of our near divorce and subsequent restoration. For many years we've resisted such invitations, not least because some of the memories are very painful even now. Certainly *Marriage Masterclass* was not the place to tell the story in detail. But our editor, Ali Hull, wisely recognised that people reading this book may want to know more about our story. So, at her prompting, we are telling our story, warts and all, in *The Hope Tree* to be published by Authentic.

The Hope Tree is the true account of the breakdown and restoration of a marriage. The breakdown might have happened to any couple but the restoration was remarkable. It came when we had been apart for three years, when we believed that our relationship was dead and when each was looking forward to a new life.

Our joint story begins with Anne, a single parent, living in a run down cottage. She was striving to gain a teaching degree to achieve a better life for herself and her two small children. Balancing study and family, Anne felt that she had been battling half her life against poverty and adversity when, unexpectedly, a long time friendship blossomed into romance. Tony, a close friend asked Anne to marry him and deeply in love, delirious with happiness, Anne believed that all her troubles were about to end.

Although the friendship had been deep and the engagement wonderful but busy, nevertheless issues began to arise between us, some even before the last crumbs of the wedding cake were brushed away. But these were ignored or buried, left to fester unresolved, in the hope that the problems would eventually disappear. They didn't. Years into the marriage, a cluster of problems caused a series of powerful emotional scenes to rip through the skin of our defences, blowing apart a relationship far more fragile than either of us had suspected.

Mistrustful of Tony's feelings, Anne thought that he no longer cared for her; even though he said that he did. Exhausted by circumstances, fearful of Tony's anger, and rejecting all Christian contact, Anne moved two hundred miles away to a new life. Desolated, Tony sank into clinical depression.

More than two years went by, during which time we had little or no contact with one another. In her new home amid the Welsh mountains, Anne's pain gradually subsided until finally she was able to hear God speaking to her once more. Meanwhile, Tony had also experienced personal healing and subsequently made a new life for himself. Thinking that our relationship was dead, he likened it to a limb that has gone gangrenous and could no longer be saved, needing to be amputated so as to allow full recovery. To this end he instructed a solicitor to begin divorce proceedings.

But Anne had come to a different place. Even though she was happy in her new situation and had gained professional esteem, she knew that the life she was living was wrong. She repented and returned to church. When the divorce papers dropped through her door she knew that it was time to seek reconciliation.

After two and a half years we arranged to meet. Tony believed that the only purpose of a meeting was to communicate forgiveness to one another and say goodbye forever. When Anne asked if it was possible to be reconciled he told her that it was no longer that simple; life had moved on for him. Both recognised that it would be easier, and certainly less painful to say our goodbyes to each other. But we also recognised that the Bible has powerful things to say about marriage. We were faced with a choice: just to claim to being disciples with a commitment to the authority of Scripture, or to live out that commitment by trying to obey Scripture – knowing that obeying would be painful, unpleasant and not what we really wanted to do at that time.

Our coming back together was as fraught as our parting but come together again we did. We had gone to the brink of divorce, even having to buy our marriage certificate back from the divorce court. Finally, after much hard work we were truly reconciled. To celebrate the first wedding anniversary of our restoration again we planted a tiny tree together, the hope tree. More than a decade on it is as strong and flourishing as our marriage.